COMPACT CD DISC
packaging and graphics

by ken pfeifer

THE BEST PROMOTIONAL AND RETAIL PACKAGING

Book Development and Editorial
KEN PFEIFER

Book Design
EILIS Mc DONNELL

Art Direction
STEPHEN BRIDGES
KEN PFEIFER

Photography
ROB HUNTLEY FOR CHROMOGRAPHICS
(Except Where Noted)

Art Production
SARA DAY

Production Management
BARBARA STATES

Typesetting
CAMERA READY TYPE & GRAPHICS

Special thanks to Jeff Rentsch and Tom King
for their support of everything leading
up to this publication. Special thanks also to
Glen Christensen of Glen Christensen & Associates,
for assistance in contact and collection.
A warm thanks finally to everyone who
participated in and contributed to this book.

First published in the United States of America by:
ROCKPORT PUBLISHERS, INC.
P.O. BOX 396
FIVE SMITH STREET
ROCKPORT, MASSACHUSETTS 01966
TELEPHONE: (508) 546-9590
FAX: (508) 546-7141
TELEX: 5106019284 ROCKORT PUB

**Distributed to the book trade and
art trade in the U.S. and Canada by:**
NORTH LIGHT, AN IMPRINT OF
F & W PUBLICATIONS
1507 DANA AVENUE
CINCINNATI, OHIO 45207
TELEPHONE: (513) 531-2222

First UK & Europe edition published by:
ROCKPORT PUBLISHERS, INC. FOR
GINGKO PRESS VERLAGS GMBH
HAMBURGERSTRASSE 180,
200 HAMBURG 76 GERMANY
TELEPHONE: 040 291425
FAX: 040 291055

Other Distribution by:
ROCKPORT PUBLISHERS, INC.
.ROCKPORT, MASSACHUSETTS 01966

ISBN 3-927258-09-1

Printed in Singapore

COMPACT DISC

CD

packaging and graphics

Gingko
PRESS

CONTENTS

PREFACE

I remember a time during the 1970s when my record collection was actually two collections: one audio and one visual. Record album packages came in all variations of shape and size, with some of the most unforgettable graphics ever.

Since the time CDs came on the market, records have all but disappeared. While graphics for CDs has continued to yield creative results, there have been relatively few advances in packaging until recently.

Now there is great variety in CD packaging, especially for promotional and limited-edition releases. In this book I present a new collection of such packaging and design. Although they are new, many of the pieces included are rare items, featured here to make such excellence in design available to more than just a select few.

I hope that this book will serve as a document of today's CD packaging, and that it will encourage production of similar material on a greater scale, to make items like these more commonly available, for all to enjoy.

Ken Pfeifer

Ken Pfeifer

INTRODUCTION

Compact discs have taken over the world of recorded music so quickly and so completely that many record-cover designers have had to rethink their entire approach seemingly overnight. The advent and ascendance of CDs brings a new challenge to designers trying to satisfy both marketing and aesthetic demands. Most important to designers is the likelihood that he or she will be working with a smaller surface. Except for box sets, some of which retain the traditional 12-by-12-inch LP format, nearly all commercially available CDs are designed in either 6-by-12 or 5-by-5 form. Such a move was distressing to vinyl loyalists — at first it seemed like reading CD liner notes would necessitate a magnifying glass — but as *COMPACT DISC PACKAGING AND GRAPHICS* makes delightfully clear, the smaller surface of CDs has not limited the field's top designers. In many ways, the new form demands of its designers more care, more precision, more imagination.

And the pop-music audience demands such expertise. For rock and roll fans, album covers have always been a crucial part of record-buying and record-enjoying. Most record company executives have always considered covers mere marketing opportunities, but designers and fans know better. As far back as the cover of RCA's first Elvis Presley album in 1956, a black and white performance shot of Elvis and his guitar covered with pink and green lettering every bit as loud as the cry we imagine coming out of the young King, inspired record packaging has been inextricable from the music inside. For most fans, from the casual to the obsessive, a rock and roll record is a product in which although the music is the most important element, it is far from the only one. A great record package satisfies more than one sense.

Now that most serious record-buyers are concentrating on CD purchases, it is impossible to over estimate the importance to fans of remarkable CD design. So it's no accident that many brilliant packages showcased in this volume originally intended only for promotional use like the *"can"* version of Keith Richards's *Talk Is Cheap* (p. 32) and the dazzling *"postcard"* configuration of R.E.M.'s *Out Of Time* (p. 28) — were quickly made available to a public that demanded them. Such sets carry a premium price, but fans are willing to pay that price when they are presented with a great package that they consider an appropriate extension of a performer's intentions. David Bowie is a performer noted as much for his visual representations of himself as his music, and when Rykodisc began its rereleases of Bowie's Seventies records with the boxed set *Sound + Vision* (p. 136) it created a monumental three-dimensional package. The innovative boxed set served as an ideal complement to the wide-ranging music inside and informed fans that the upcoming reissue campaign would be worth following. On the other extreme, no one will argue that the Simpsons's *"Do the Bartman"* (p. 102) is essential rap, yet Geffen's package for the CD single is as kinetic and dashing as the iconoclastic animated family. The package works, and then adds weight to what's inside.

Until recently, the standard for commercial CDs in the United States is a 6-by-12 disposable longbox enclosing a 5-by-5 jewel box with a booklet and the CD. (In nearly all other countries, the 6-by-12 has already been disposed of, and CDs are sold in shrink-wrapped jewel boxes.) The many worthy environmental arguments against the 6-by-12 have finally won out, and there are currently many innovative attempts underway toward a new standard. The Digipak, the Digitrak, the Eco-Pak, the Laserfile, and the Smart-Pak all hold promise, though the billions of already-sold jewel boxes suggest that any new standard not built around a jewel box will meet heavy consumer resistance. Although designers need to operate under market constraints — few labels are still releasing 12-by-12 box sets because LP-sized bins have disappeared from many shops — throughout *COMPACT DISC PACKAGING AND GRAPHICS* we see the work of artists striking a balance between no predetermined standards (room for full creativity, no constraints on size) and the real world.

CDs have only been in record stores since 1983, yet the advances in CD packaging in that period have been stunning. For example, CD booklets started as one sheet of paper with ads on the back side, now such booklets, as long as 128 pages, include written and photographic essays that add substantial value to the music. When CDs began to take over in the late Eighties, some vinyl loyalists feared that record design was a dead art. More than only allaying such fears, *COMPACT DISC PACKAGING AND GRAPHICS* is a definitive presentation of the most innovative gains in the CD's first decade; none of us can imagine how much farther we will travel in the next ten years.

Jimmy Guterman

Jimmy Guterman

Jimmy Guterman is the author of five books, among them *Rockin' My Life Away* and *12 Days On The Road*. He lives in Massachusetts.

PROMOTIONAL

A significant amount of design and packaging for CDs is done for promotional use only rather than for retail sales. These "Pro-CDs" represent some of the most creative ideas and design for music media, providing a creative outlet for art directors at labels that was until recently unrealized.

WARM AND TENDER

OLIVIA NEWTON-JOHN

LABEL

GEFFEN

ART DIRECTION

GABRIELLE RAUMBERGER

DESIGN

LARRY VIGON STUDIO

PHOTOGRAPHY

ALBERTO TOLOT

NANCY MANNING

The use of modest, recycled materials does not hinder the visual impact of this environmentally-conscious package.

JULIA FORDHAM
MANHATTAN SKYLINE
AND OTHER STORIES

MANHATTAN SKYLINE
JULIA FORDHAM

LABEL
VIRGIN RECORDS
ART DIRECTION
MELANIE NISSEN
DESIGN
TIMOTHY EAMES

This package features an excellent die-cut pattern playing off the title. The skyline design is a brilliant finish to an already elegant promotion.

PLAYING THE ORCHESTRA

RIUICHI SAKAMOTO

LABEL
VIRGIN RECORDS

ART DIRECTION
SHINRO OHTAKE

DESIGN
KATSUHIRO KINOSHITA

PHOTOGRAPHY
MASATAKA NAKANO

The box installation includes hand-punched holes, with small pebbles trapped inside.

PUMP

AEROSMITH

LABEL

GEFFEN

ART DIRECTION

KIM CHAMPAGNE

**GABRIELLE
RAUMBERGER**

DESIGN

KIM CHAMPAGNE

BAND PHOTOGRAPHY

NORMAN SEEFF

TRUCK
PHOTOGRAPHY

**AMERICAN STOCK
PHOTOGRAPHY**

GAS PUMP
PHOTOGRAPHY

SOL LIBSON

**UNIVERSITY OF
LOUISVILLE PHOTO
ARCHIVES**

LOGO RENDERING

ANDY ENGEL

TATTOO DESIGN

MARK RYDEN

This leather-bound package includes a slipcase. The cover stamping complements the visual quality of the leather.

WHAT IT TAKES
AEROSMITH

LABEL
GEFFEN
ART DIRECTION
SAMANTHA HART
DESIGN
**GABRIELLE
RAUMBERGER**

PHOTO COURTESY WARNER BROS.

This single from the Pump album is modeled after the Pump
promotional CD. The embossed card stock package unfolds to reveal
the disc as well as a poster inside.

SEX CYMBAL

SHEILA E.

LABEL
WARNER BROTHERS
ART DIRECTION
JERI HEIDEN
DESIGN
SARAJO FRIEDEN
PHOTOGRAPHY
PHILIP DIXON

TOO LEGIT TO 'QUIT

HAMMER

LABEL
CAPITOL
ART DIRECTION
TOMMY STEELE
DESIGN
STEPHEN WALKER
PHOTOGRAPHY
ANNIE LEIBOVITZ

This elaborate promotion features a metal Digipak cover.

CAPITOL LEANING TOWER PIZZA

VARIOUS ARTISTS

LABEL
CAPITOL
ART DIRECTION
TOMMY STEELE
DESIGN
JIM HEIMANN
PHOTOGRAPHY
LARRY DuPONT

Here, the art director has emulated a typical take-out pizza box, paying close attention to detail. The finishing touch is the grease-soaked area printed on the bottom panel. This and the package on the overleaf demonstrate Capitol's unique approach to various artists' collections.

CAPITOL TASTY
TOWER TREATS
VARIOUS ARTISTS

LABEL
CAPITOL
ART DIRECTION
TOMMY STEELE
DESIGN
JIM HEIMANN
PHOTOGRAPHY
LARRY DuPONT

*ROCK & ROLL
STRATEGY*

38 SPECIAL

LABEL

A & M

ART DIRECTION

NORMAN MOORE

DESIGN

NORMAN MOORE

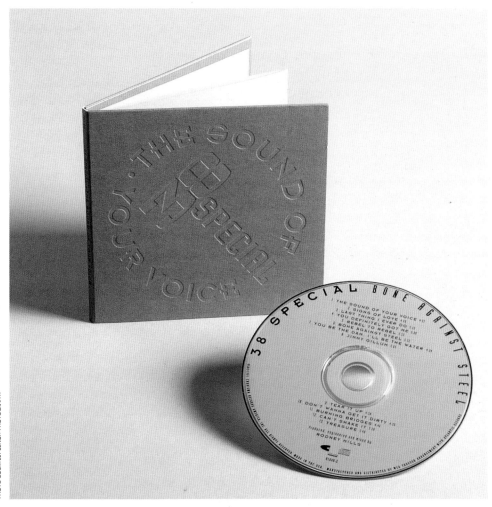

*THE SOUND OF YOUR
VOICE*

38 SPECIAL

LABEL

CHARISMA

ART DIRECTION

NORMAN MOORE

DESIGN

NORMAN MOORE

FLYING COWBOYS
RICKIE LEE JONES

LABEL
GEFFEN
ART DIRECTION
SAMANTHA HART
DESIGN
praxis
PHOTOGRAPHY
DEWEY NICKS
ILLUSTRATION
**JOSE ESTEBAN
MARTINEZ**

CRITICS HAVE DESCRIBED MARIA McKEE AS
"IRREPRESSIBLE," PRAISING HER "COMMANDING
PRESENCE" AND "POWERFULLY PURE VOICE." HER
WORK WITH THE BAND LONE JUSTICE WAS HERALDED
BY BOTH REVIEWERS AND FANS. NOW, WORKING WITH
PRODUCER MITCHELL FROOM — WHOSE CREDITS
INCLUDE WORK WITH LOS LOBOS, CROWDED HOUSE AND
PAUL McCARTNEY — SHE RELEASES HER SOLO DEBUT
[GE]FFEN RECORDS. FOR THE FIRST TIME,
[MARIA] McKEE STANDS ALONE.

MARIA McKEE

LABEL
GEFFEN
ART DIRECTION
JONAS
LIVINGSTON
DESIGN
MARIA DeGRASSI

Radio Song
Losing My Religion
Low
Near Wild Heaven
Endgame
Shiny Happy People
Belong
Half A World Away
Texarkana
Country Feedback
Me In Honey

R.E.M.
OUT OF TIME

OUT OF TIME
R.E.M.

LABEL
WARNER BROTHERS
ART DIRECTION
TOM RECCHION
MICHAEL STIPE
DESIGN
TOM RECCHION
MICHAEL STIPE
BAND PHOTOGRAPHY
FRANK OCKENFELS
OTHER
PHOTOGRAPHY
PLANT DETAILS #3:
YELLOW SEASCAPE
WITH FILM AND
WOOD BLOCK
**DOUG & MIKE
STARN**
ED ROGERS
**DAVID
GREENBERGER/
DUPLEX PLANET**

ILLUSTRATION
BEN KATCHOR
HAND LETTERING
ED ROGERS
COMPUTER
GRAPHICS
TOM RECCHION
COLLAGE
TOM RECCHION
MICHAEL STIPE

WITHOUT A NET
GRATEFUL DEAD

LABEL
ARISTA
ART DIRECTION
CAROLYN QUAN
DESIGN
CAROLYN QUAN
PHOTOGRAPHY
KEN FRIEDMAN
SUSANA MILLMAN
JOHN WERNER
ILLUSTRATION
RICK GRIFFIN
**MIKIO/WILLIAM
GIESE**

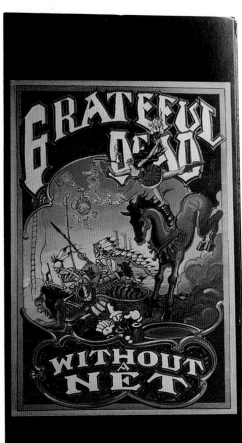

FREAK SHOW
BULLET BOYS

LABEL
WARNER BROTHERS
ART DIRECTION
KIM CHAMPAGNE
JEFF GOLD
JIM LADWIG
DESIGN
KIM CHAMPAGNE
ILLUSTRATION
DAVID B. McMACKEN
PHOTOGRAPHY
AARON RAPOPORT

Unfolding from a simple square package, the accordion-folds form the shape of a camera. The combination of the old-fashioned shape and the contemporary graphics creates a most unique effect.

TALK IS CHEAP
KEITH RICHARDS

LABEL
VIRGIN RECORDS
ART DIRECTION
MELANIE NISSEN
DESIGN
TIMOTHY EAMES
PHOTOGRAPHY
SANTE D'ORAZIO
ALASTAIR THAIN

This can includes an
entire full-length
album of material on
three three-inch
singles.

RECYCLER

ZZ TOP

LABEL

WARNER BROTHERS

ART DIRECTION

JEFF GOLD
KIM CHAMPAGNE

DESIGN

KIM CHAMPAGNE

ILLUSTRATION &
LOGO

BARRY JACKSON

PHOTOGRAPHY

**WALTAIRE "MOJO
PHOTO" BALDWIN**

**ROBERT "MINT
MAN" JOHNSON**

MISS "X" TINE

One of the best-known packages in this collection, the Recycler CD
includes metal man-hole cover material for the front and back.

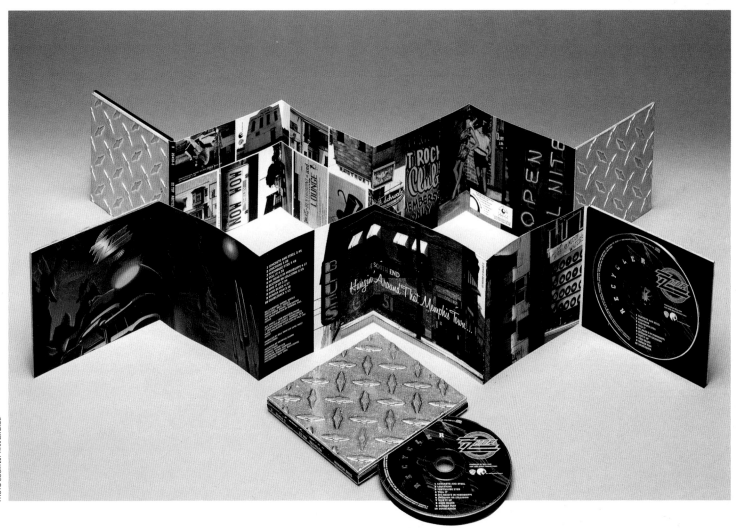

HOUSE OF HOPE
TONI CHILDS

LABEL
A & M
ART DIRECTION
LEN PELTIER
DESIGN
LEN PELTIER
PHOTOGRAPHY
CRAIG ROPER

The various layers of printed papers, cardboard, and insulation material in this package make it an appealing, *"low-tech"* piece.

*REFUGEES OF THE
HEART*

STEVE WINWOOD

LABEL

VIRGIN

ART DIRECTION

MELANIE NISSEN

DESIGN

MIKE FINK

PHOTOGRAPHY

**THE DOUGLAS
BROTHERS**

COCTEAU TWINS
COCTEAU TWINS

LABEL
CAPITOL
ART DIRECTION
**VAUGHN OLIVER/
PAUL WEST FOR
4 A.D.**
BOX COORDINATION
**TOMMY STEELE/
JULIA CAMPBELL
FOR CAPITOL**

DEAD IN A DECK
GRATEFUL DEAD

LABEL
ARISTA
ART DIRECTION
MAUDE GILMAN
DESIGN
MAUDE GILMAN

LOWDOWN AND DIRTY
FOREIGNER

LABEL
ATLANTIC
ART DIRECTION
BOB DEFRIN
DESIGN
BOB DEFRIN

The outer-casing of this Digipak is made from actual vinyl records.

*di*VINYLS

diVINYLS

LABEL
VIRGIN
ART DIRECTION
MELANIE NISSEN
DESIGN
INGE SCHAAP
PHOTOGRAPHY
MELANIE NISSEN
TORKIL GUDNASON

STEP BY STEP

**NEW KIDS ON THE
BLOCK**

LABEL
SONY
ART DIRECTION
**CHRISTOPHER
AUSTUPCHUCK**
DESIGN
MARK BURDETT
PHOTOGRAPHY
CHIP SIMONS

FAMILY STYLE
**VAUGHAN
BROTHERS**

LABEL
SONY
ART DIRECTION
TONY SELLARI
DESIGN
TONY SELLARI
PHOTOGRAPHY
LEE CRUM

WEATHERBOX

DAVID SYLVIAN

LABEL
VIRGIN

ART DIRECTION
**RUSSELL MILLS
AND DAVE
COPPENHALL (mc²)**

DESIGN
**RUSSELL MILLS
AND DAVE
COPPENHALL (mc²)**

PHOTOGRAPHY
DAVID BUCKLAND

THAT'S WHY
JELLYFISH

LABEL
CHARISMA
ART DIRECTION
STEVE SAMIOF
DESIGN
RON MECKLER
PHOTOGRAPHY
PETER DARLEY MILLER

Affectionately called the *"Jelly-Pak,"* this plastic package includes a jelly-like liquid with confetti suspended inside.

BEHIND THE MASK
FLEETWOOD MAC

LABEL
WARNER BROTHERS
ART DIRECTION
JERI HEIDEN
DESIGN
JERI HEIDEN
PHOTOGRAPHY
D. GORTON

LOVE HURTS

CHER

LABEL
GEFFEN
ART DIRECTION
MARGO CHASE
DESIGN
MARGO CHASE
SAMANTHA HART

LUCK OF THE DRAW
BONNIE RAITT

LABEL
CAPITOL
ART DIRECTION
TOMMY STEELE
DESIGN
JEFFERY FEY
PHOTOGRAPHY
MERLYN ROSENBERG
LETTERING
MARGO CHASE

NIGHT RIDE HOME
JONI MITCHELL

LABEL
GEFFEN
ART DIRECTION
JANET WOLSBORN
DESIGN
GLEN CHRISTENSEN
PHOTOGRAPHY
JONI MITCHELL

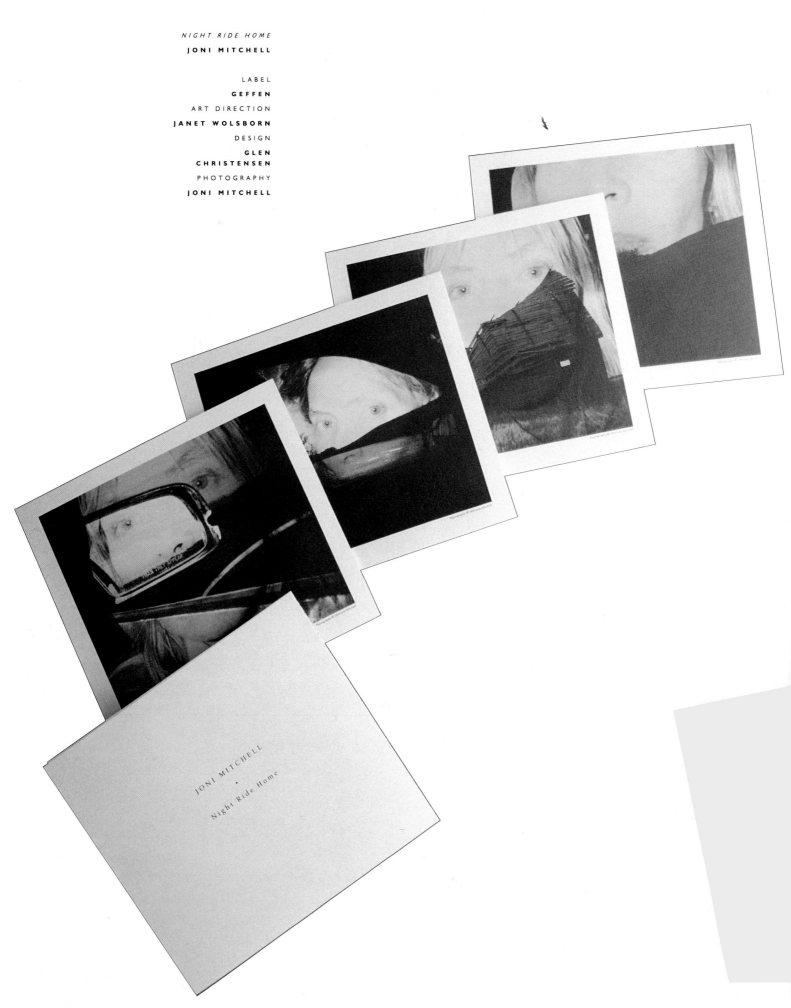

This echoes the form of a photographer's promotional package, with original art by the recording artist.

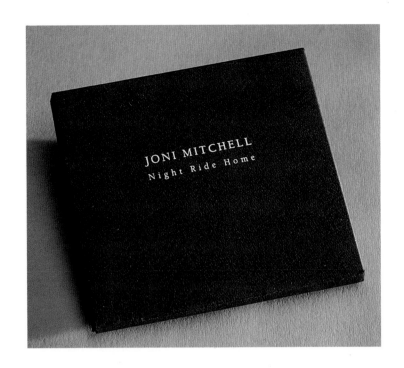

WOODFACE

CROWDED HOUSE

LABEL
CAPITOL
ART DIRECTION
TOMMY STEELE
DESIGN
STEPHEN WALKER
BAND PHOTOGRAPHY
DENNIS KEELEY
STILL LIFE
PHOTOGRAPHY
PETE McARTHUR
LETTERFORMS
TIMOTHY EAMES
COVER
ILLUSTRATION
JULIA CAMPBELL

SUPERSTITION

**SIOUXSIE & THE
BANSHEES**

LABEL
GEFFEN
ART DIRECTION
SAMANTHA HART
JIM LADWIG
DESIGN
SAMANTHA HART

SUPERSTITION

**SIOUXSIE & THE
BANSHEES**

LABEL
GEFFEN
ART DIRECTION
SAMANTHA HART
JIM LADWIG
DESIGN
SAMANTHA HART

"I definitely think that people would buy these packages [when sold in retail stores]. A lot of it's in the marketing, because consumer awareness has not yet risen in this field. Additionally, it's important that 'special' packages are released simultaneously with the regular retail package because the initial influx of customers going to the stores to purchase a new release are the strongest base of 'fans' who would be particularly interested in additional photographs or graphics which make it a collectible item."

SAMANTHA HART, GEFFEN RECORDS

SLIP OF THE TONGUE
WHITESNAKE

LABEL
GEFFEN
PACKAGING
CONCEPT
SAMANTHA HART
ART DIRECTION
HUGH SYME
DESIGN
**GABRIELLE
RAUMBERGER
SAMANTHA HART**
ILLUSTRATION
HUGH SYME

*IT'S A BEAUTIFUL
THING*
**IT'S A BEAUTIFUL
THING**

LABEL
POLYGRAM
ART DIRECTION
**MICHAEL BAYS
ALLI TRUCH**
DESIGN
**MICHAEL BAYS
ALLI TRUCH**

CRADLE OF LOVE
BILLY IDOL

LABEL
CHRYSALIS
ART DIRECTION
PETER CORRISTON
DESIGN
RANDALL MARTIN
PHOTOGRAPHY
**GEORGE KERRIGAN
AGUILERA-
HELLWEG**

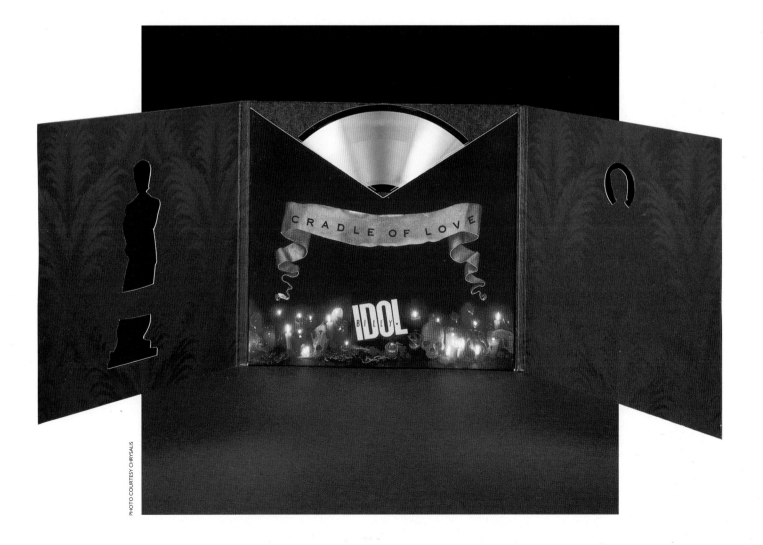

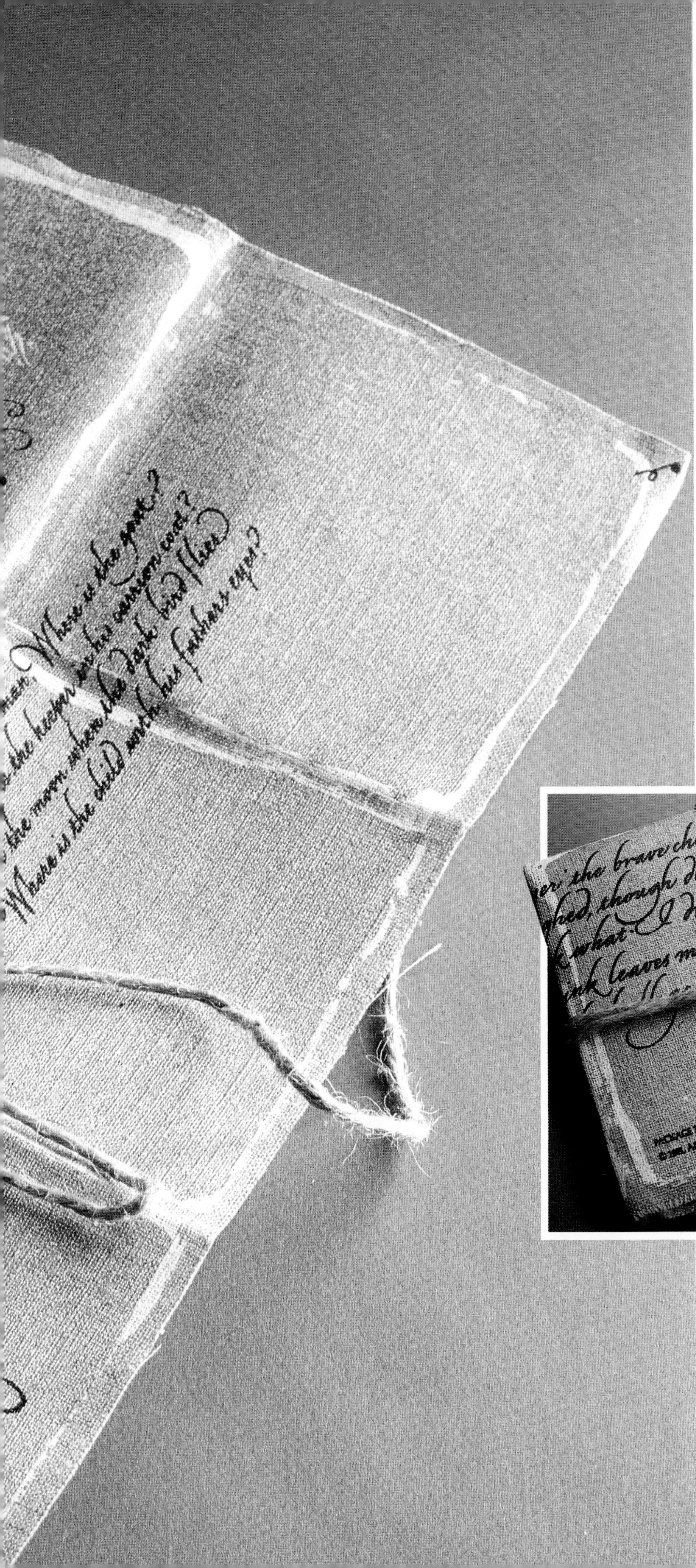

THE SOUL CAGES
STING

LABEL
A & M
ART DIRECTION
LEN PELTIER
DESIGN
LEN PELTIER

LABEL

VIRGIN

ART DIRECTION

MELANIE NISSEN

DESIGN

INGE SCHAAP

PHOTOGRAPHY

ANDRÉ LANSEL

The inside card, with the disc attached, is spring-loaded with a rubber band. When removed, the disc snaps forward revealing the printed word *"Surprise."*

THE IMMACULATE
COLLECTION

MADONNA

LABEL
WARNER BROTHERS
ART DIRECTION
JERI HEIDEN
DESIGN
JERI HEIDEN
JOHN HEIDEN
PHOTOGRAPHY
HERB RITTS

CHASE THE CLOUDS
KEEDY

LABEL
ARISTA
ART DIRECTION
ELISA MARSHALL
DESIGN
ELISA MARSHALL
PHOTOGRAPHY
**RANDEE ST.
NICHOLAS**

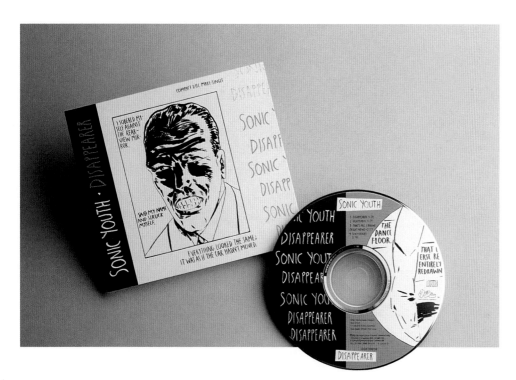

DISAPPEARER
SONIC YOUTH

LABEL
GEFFEN
PACKAGING
CONCEPT
SAMANTHA HART
ART DIRECTION
KEVIN REAGAN
DESIGN
KEVIN REAGAN
ILLUSTRATION
RAYMOND PETTIBONE

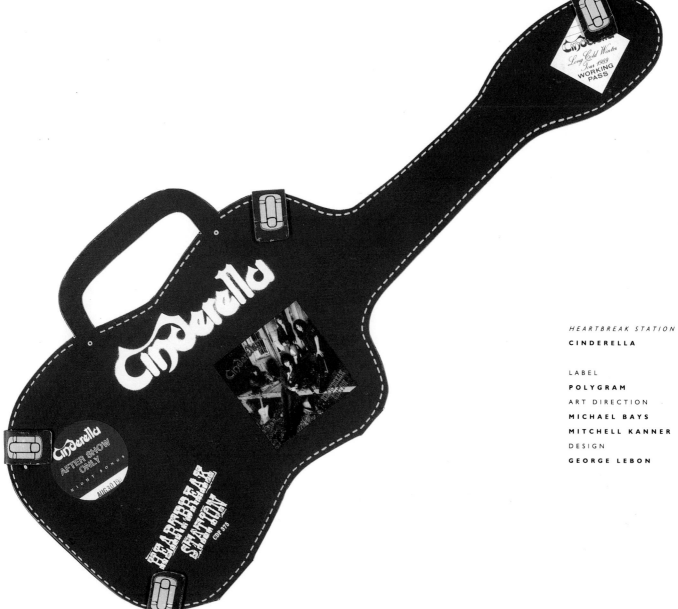

HEARTBREAK STATION
CINDERELLA

LABEL
POLYGRAM
ART DIRECTION
MICHAEL BAYS
MITCHELL KANNER
DESIGN
GEORGE LEBON

FROM THE HEART
TOMMY PAGE

LABEL
WARNER BROTHERS
ART DIRECTION
MARY ANN DIBS
DESIGN
MARY ANN DIBS
PHOTOGRAPHY
ALBERT SANCHEZ

*SOLD ME DOWN THE
RIVER*
THE ALARM

LABEL
IRS
ART DIRECTION
HUGH BROWN
DESIGN
GREG HORTON
PHOTOGRAPHY
RUSSEL YOUNG

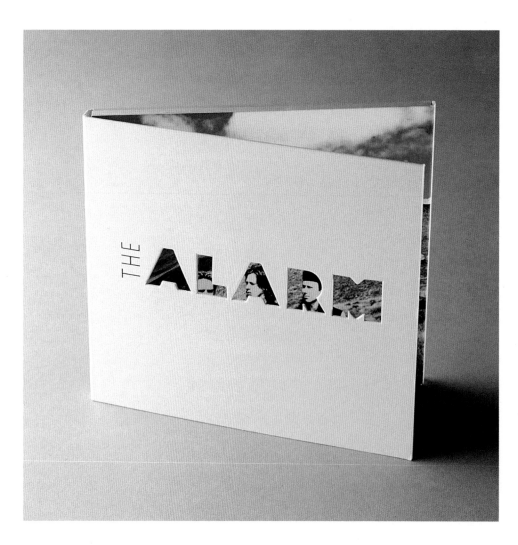

GOODBYE JUMBO

WORLD PARTY

LABEL
CHRYSALIS
ART DIRECTION
PETER CORRISTON
DESIGN
HUBERT KRETSCHMAR
PHOTOGRAPHY
HUBERT KRETSCHMAR

The die-cutting of the Digipak cover allows for the disc to be rotated. The printed image on the disc consists of small symbols that show through the die-cut holes.

*WORLD OUTSIDE
YOUR WINDOW*

TANITA TIKARAM

LABEL

EAST-WEST

DESIGN

T&CP ASSOCIATES

PHOTOGRAPHY

TERRY O'NEILL

*LITTLE SISTER
LEAVING TOWN*

TANITA TIKARAM

LABEL

EAST-WEST

DESIGN

T&CP ASSOCIATES

ILLUSTRATION

T&CP ASSOCIATES

PHOTOGRAPHY

**DEBORAH
FEINGOLD**

*WE ALMOST GOT IT
TOGETHER*

TANITA TIKARAM

LABEL

EAST-WEST

DESIGN

T&CP ASSOCIATES

ILLUSTRATION

T&CP ASSOCIATES

PHOTOGRAPHY

**DEBORAH
FEINGOLD**

TANITA
TIKARAM
·
LITTLE
SISTER
LEAVING
TOWN

TANITA TIKARAM · WE ALMOST GOT IT TOGETHER

TANITA TIKARAM
world outside your window

Collectors Edition 4 Track CD
Includes Live Songs
& Photographs

*REFLECTIONS OF
PASSION*

YANNI

LABEL

PRIVATE

ART DIRECTION

**ICON, LOS
ANGELES AND
LONDON**

DESIGN

**ICON, LOS
ANGELES AND
LONDON**

PHOTOGRAPHY

LYNN GOLDSMITH

LOVE LIKE THIS

KENNEDY ROSE

LABEL

IRS

ART DIRECTION

HUGH BROWN

DESIGN

HUGH BROWN

WORKBOOK
BOB MOULD

LABEL
VIRGIN
ART DIRECTION
MELANIE NISSEN
DESIGN
TIM STEADMAN
COVER ART
MICHAEL COVINGTON
PHOTOGRAPHY
MARC NORBERG

ANIMAL LOGIC
ANIMAL LOGIC

LABEL
IRS
ART DIRECTION
HUGH BROWN
DESIGN
HUGH BROWN

COLLECTION BOX

THE CHURCH

LABEL
ARISTA
ART DIRECTION
MAUDE GILMAN
DESIGN
MAUDE GILMAN
PHOTOGRAPHY
JOHN HALPERN

*VAN MORRISON'S
MERCURY MUSIC*
VAN MORRISON

LABEL
POLYGRAM
ART DIRECTION
BEN ARGUETA

HOOKED
GREAT WHITE

LABEL
CAPITOL
ART DIRECTION
TOMMY STEELE
DESIGN
TOMMY STEELE

"Special packaging has really opened up the design aspect in a big way. We're less limited than we have been, by only designing the booklet and inlay. This adds a concept again to the design process."

TOMMY STEELE,
CAPITOL RECORDS

CRUEL, CRAZY
BEAUTIFUL WORLD
JOHNNY CLEGG &
SAVUKA

LABEL
CAPITOL
ART DIRECTION
TOMMY STEELE
DESIGN
CHUCK AMES
PHOTOGRAPHY
DOUG HYUN

*INTELLIGENT
HOODLUM*

**INTELLIGENT
HOODLUM**

LABEL
A&M
ART DIRECTION
LEN PELTIER
DESIGN
**LEN PELTIER
ROWAN MOORE**

FLASHPOINT

**THE ROLLING
STONES**

ART DIRECTION
VIVID ID
JOHN WARWICKER
DESIGN
VIVID ID
JOHN WARWICKER

This promotion
includes a CD as
well as a video
single.

Go Dog Go Music BMI
From the Giant album ON
THE WINGS OF DIRTY
ANGELS (4/2-24400) ⓟ ⓒ 1990
Giant Records, manufactured
exclusively by Reprise Records, a Time
Warner Company. Mfg. by Discovery Systems.
PRO-CD-4413

PROMOTION ONLY. NOT FOR SALE.. MADE IN USA

TERRELL
SOULS OF PIRATES
(Album Version) 3:37
PRODUCED by
HAWK &
terrell

*ON THE WINGS OF
DIRTY ANGELS*

TERRELL

LABEL
WARNER BROTHERS
ART DIRECTION
KIM CHAMPAGNE
DESIGN
KIM CHAMPAGNE
PHOTGRAPHY
MARK ABRAHAMS

PASSPORT
TINA TURNER

LABEL
CAPITOL
ART DIRECTION
TOMMY STEELE
BILL BURKS
DESIGN
GLENN SAKAMOTO
PHOTOGRAPHY
PETER LINDBERGH
HERB RITTS
ILLUSTRATION
ANDY ENGEL

"We hope to continue producing special packaging. A special edition sold at retail helps defray the cost of promotion. We run maybe 10,000 to 15,000 units, which can be an expensive promotion if we don't offset it with retail sales. Of course, if we did it for every artist, it would no longer be special, so we still have to be a little selective."

TOMMY STEELE, CAPITOL RECORDS

COCA-COLA USA 1991
SUMMER POP MUSIC
PROMOTION

ART DIRECTION
JANE COKER
FRANK GOLLEY
DESIGN
JANE COKER
FRANK GOLLEY

MIGHTY LIKE A ROSE
ELVIS COSTELLO

LABEL
WARNER BROTHERS
DIGI-PAK DESIGN
DIRK WALTER
BOOKLET DESIGN
MIKE KRAGE
EAMMON SINGER
PHOTOGRAPHY
AMELIA STEIN

PHOTO COURTESY WARNER BROS.

STRENGTH IN
NUMBERS

38 SPECIAL

LABEL
A&M
ART DIRECTION
NORMAN MOORE
DESIGN
NORMAN MOORE
PHOTOGRAPHY
DENNIS KEELEY

24 HOUR MAN
LOCK UP

LABEL
GEFFEN
ART DIRECTION
KEVIN REAGAN
DESIGN
KEVIN REAGAN
ILLUSTRATION
BRIAN GRILLO

AFFECTION

LISA STANSFIELD

LABEL

ARISTA

ART DIRECTION

SUSAN MENDOLA

DESIGN

MICHAEL-NASH
ASSOCIATES

SUSAN MENDOLA

PHOTOGRAPHY

KATE GARNER

ONE BRIGHT DAY

**ZIGGY MARLEY
AND THE MELODY
MAKERS**

LABEL
VIRGIN
ART DIRECTION
JEFF AYEROFF
DESIGN
INGE SCHAAP

DEADICATED

VARIOUS ARTISTS

LABEL

ARISTA

ART DIRECTION

SUSAN MENDOLA

DESIGN

SUSAN MENDOLA

PHOTOGRAPHY

DAVID BLANK

GREG GORMAN

LESTER COHEN

TERRY O'NEILL

NICK VACARRO

VICTORIA PEARSON-CAMERON

JEFF KATZ

MICHAEL LAVINE

CHRIS BUCK/ IMPACT VISUALS

DENNIS KEELEY

DEBORAH FEINGOLD

WILLIAM COUPON

KEVIN WESTENBERG

ILLUSTRATION

MIKIO/WILLIAM GIESE

This package, printed in recycled paper, characterizes the earthy roots of the recording artist.

The new
Squeeze
album
is called
SQUEEZE
PLAY

2/26644-dj

SQUEEZE
PLAY

PLAY
SQUEEZE

LABEL
WARNER BROTHERS
ART DIRECTOR
JEFF GOLD
DESIGNER
KIM CHAMPAGNE
PHOTOGRAPHER
ENRIQUE
BADULESCU

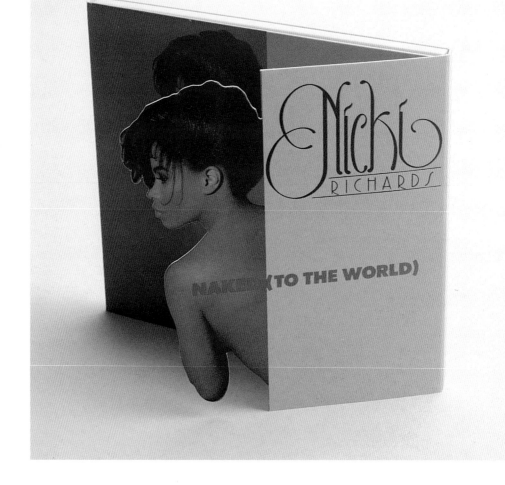

LOU REED/JOHN CALE

SONGS FOR DRELLA

SONGS FOR DRELLA
**LOU REED/
JOHN CALE**

LABEL
WARNER BROTHERS
ART DIRECTION
**TOM RECCHION
SYLVIA REED**
DESIGN
**TOM RECCHION
SYLVIA REED**
PHOTO OF
ANDY WARHOL
BILLY NAME
PHOTO OF
LOU REED AND
JOHN CALE
JAMES HAMILTON
BOOKLET
PHOTOGRAPHY
**NAT FINKELSTEIN
GERARD MALANGA
STEPHEN SHORE
ISE VALERIS**

"I love packages that are playful and that comment on the period during which they are released... I like moving parts. Some of my best ideas come from playing with my seven year old daughter, Vignette. Children's products are simple, yet very inventive."

SAMANTHA HART, GEFFEN RECORDS

DO THE BARTMAN

THE SIMPSONS

LABEL

GEFFEN

PACKAGING
CONCEPT

SAMANTHA HART

ART DIRECTION

MILI SMYTHE

DESIGN

BILL MERRYFIELD

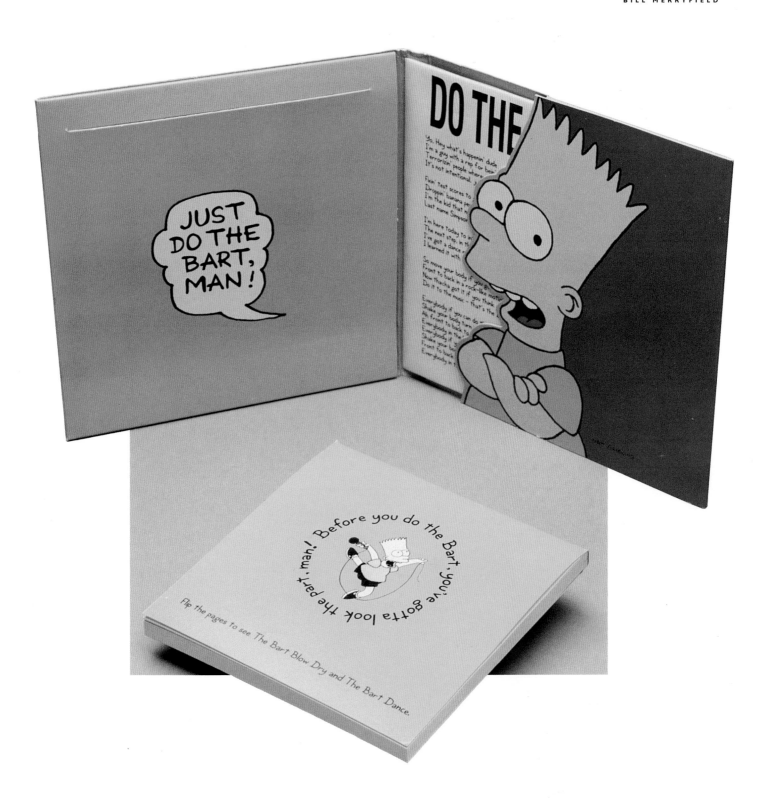

BRIGADE
HEART

LABEL
CAPITOL
ART DIRECTION
NORMAN MOORE
DESIGN
NORMAN MOORE

The graphics in this package are based on a military insignia, taking off 1960's Swiss corporate symbols.

BAD ANIMALS
HEART

LABEL
CAPITOL
ART DIRECTION
NORMAN MOORE
DESIGN
NORMAN MOORE

MICHIGAN
KIARA

LABEL
ARISTA
ART DIRECTION
SUSAN MENDOLA
DESIGN
SUSAN MENDOLA
PHOTOGRAPHY
ROBERT LEWIS

SALTWATER

JULIAN LENNON

LABEL
ATLANTIC
ART DIRECTION
JODI ROVIN
DESIGN
Ph.D
PHOTOGRAPHY
MARK HANAUER

STRESS
STRESS

LABEL
WARNER BROTHERS
ART DIRECTION
JEFF GOLD
DESIGN
GREG ROSS
PHOTOGRAPHY
ENRIQUE BADALESCU

The cover of this Digipak is heat-sensitive, revealing brighter colors when touched by warm hands.

PHOTO COURTESY WARNER BROS.

LIBERTY
DURAN DURAN

LABEL
CAPITOL
ART DIRECTION
TOMMY STEELE
DESIGN
RICHARD EVANS

COOL JERK

GO GO'S

LABEL

IRS

ART DIRECTION

NORMAN MOORE

DESIGN

NORMAN MOORE

PHOTO COURTESY BENOIT PHOTOGRAPHY

PERFECT VIEW

THE GRACES

LABEL

A & M

ART DIRECTION

NORMAN MOORE

DESIGN

NORMAN MOORE

PHOTOGRAPHY

MICHAEL MILLER

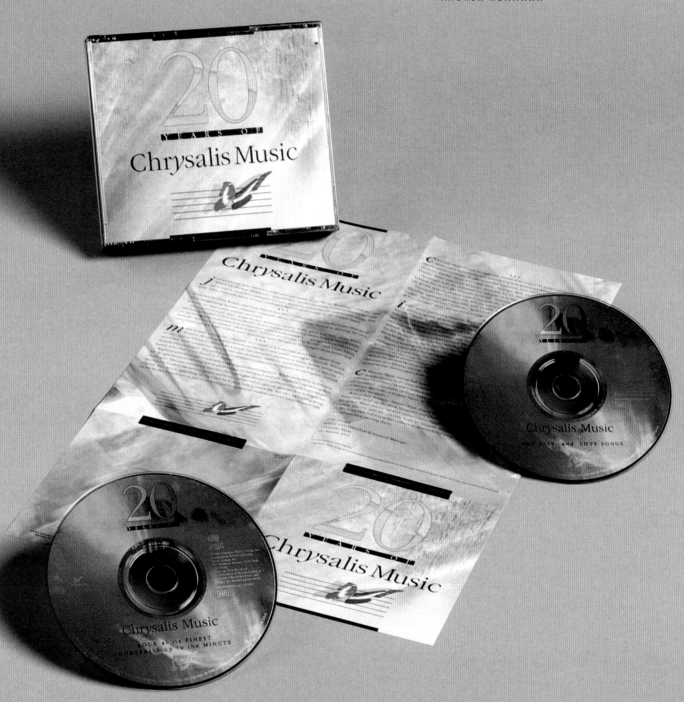

20 YEARS OF
CHRYSALIS MUSIC
VARIOUS ARTISTS

LABEL
CHRYSALIS
ART DIRECTION
RANDALL MARTIN
ANDREA HEMMANN
DESIGN
RANDALL MARTIN
ANDREA HEMMANN

There is a variety of packaging types used for retail sales. Packaging used since the inception of CDs in the early 1980s is now making way for a new generation of packaging. While this is of great interest to package designers, it has also produced exciting opportunities for grahpic designers. The future of state-of-the-art packaging for CDs holds new and promising options for designers and art directors.

STANDARD PACKAGING TYPES

In the U.S., CD's are sold in a number of different types of packaging, depending on the label and manufacturer. These packaging types represent retail packaging to date.

THE JEWEL BOX

The jewel box has been until recently the basic building block of CD packaging. Jewel boxes come in two types: one box designed for a full-length CD, and another designed for the maxi-single. The jewel box includes a removable booklet or folded card (which becomes the front *"cover"* art), along with a tray card (which comprises the side and back panels). The disc itself may be silkscreened on the non-playable side. Process screening can result in inconsistent registration throughout the entire run, so this is sometimes avoided. Nonetheless, some of the most original artwork has been produced for silkscreened CD's. Outside the U.S., most CD's are generally sold in a shrinkwrapped jewel box. The U.S. has seen several types of other packaging, shown in these pages.

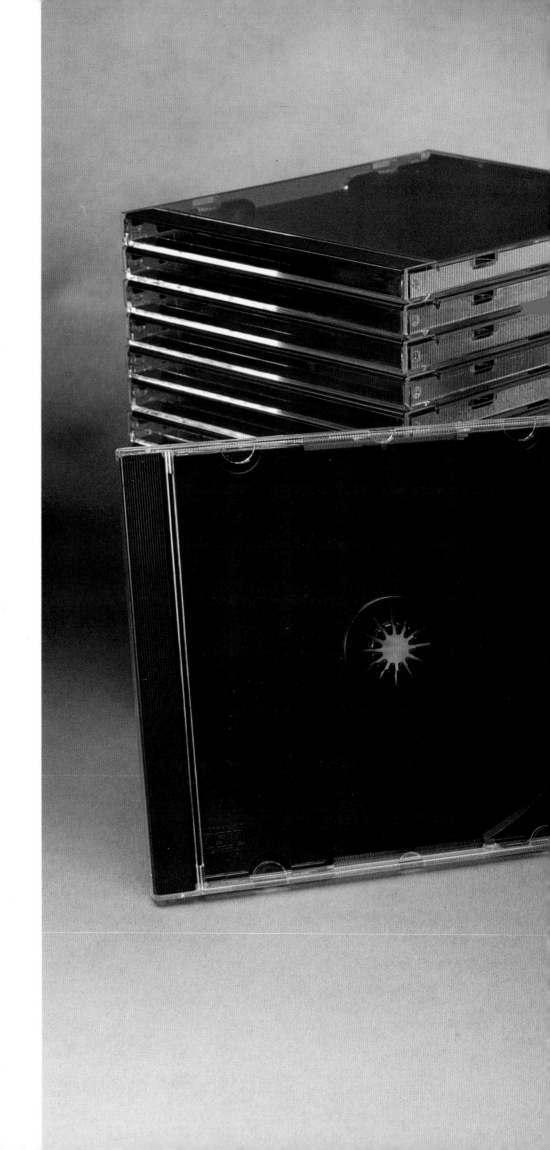

Full-length CD (r) and Maxi-single jewel boxes.

THE LONGBOX

The longbox has been one of the more enduring of CD packaging types. Designed to continue the large-size format favored by a (then) record-oriented industry, this six-inch by twelve-inch cardboard box accommodates a jewel box in the bottom-half, with the upper-half filled out with additional corrugations in the cardboard. While designers have used this large format to their best advantage, the trend at labels is to do away with the longbox for environmental and economical reasons. The campaign to eliminate longboxes is still growing, against the favor of retailers who like the longbox's uniformity for shelving purposes. While the longbox will not disappear tomorrow, its phasing-out has already begun, spawning new ideas and innovations in CD packaging.

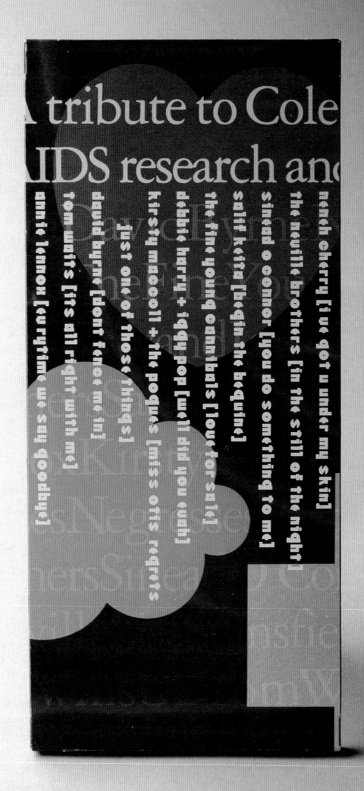

RED HOT & BLUE
VARIOUS ARTISTS

LABEL
CHRYSALIS
ART DIRECTION
HELENE SILVERMAN
DESIGN
FRANK GARGIULO

SOUND + VISION

DAVID BOWIE

LABEL
RYKODISC
ART DIRECTION
**ROGER GORMAN &
ASSOCIATES/
REINER DESIGN
CONSULTANTS**
DESIGN
**ROGER GORMAN &
ASSOCIATES/
REINER DESIGN
CONSULTANTS**

THE SPIN

THE SPIN

LABEL
DRAGON STREET
ART DIRECTION
DAVID DENNARD
DESIGN
**KARLA BARFIELD
DAVID DENNARD**

UNION

YES

LABEL
ARISTA
ART DIRECTION
CAROLYN QUAN
DESIGN
ROGER DEAN
ILLUSTRATION
ROGER DEAN

THE LONGBOX

The longbox has been one of the more enduring of CD packaging types. Designed to continue the large-size format favored by a (then) record-oriented industry, this six-inch by twelve-inch cardboard box accommodates a jewel box in the bottom-half, with the upper-half filled out with additional corrugations in the cardboard. While designers have used this large format to their best advantage, the trend at labels is to do away with the long-box for environmental and economical reasons. The campaign to eliminate longboxes is still growing, against the favor of retailers who like the long-box's uniformity for shelving purposes. While the longbox will not disappear tomorrow, its phasing-out has already begun, spawning new ideas and innovations in CD packaging.

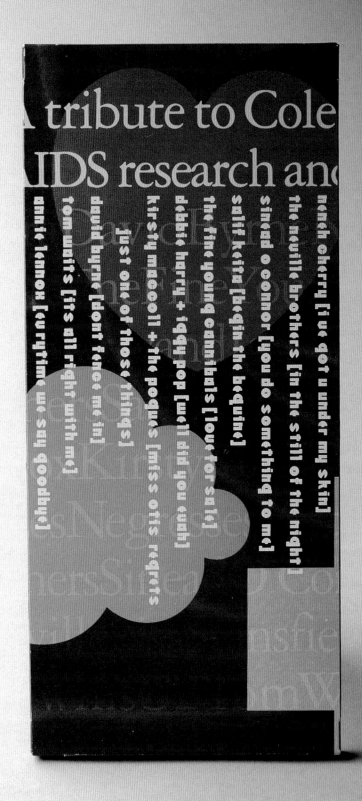

RED HOT & BLUE
VARIOUS ARTISTS

LABEL
CHRYSALIS
ART DIRECTION
HELENE SILVERMAN
DESIGN
FRANK GARGIULO

HITS OF THE 70'S

**CARIBBEAN
TAPIOCA**

LABEL
TAPIOCA
ART DIRECTION
**MARY BETH ZEITZ
DISCMAKERS**
DESIGN
**MARY BETH ZEITZ
DISCMAKERS**
ILLUSTRATION
**MARY BETH ZEITZ
DISCMAKERS**

THE BUBBLE PACK

The bubble pack is a popular package, especially for smaller labels and low-budget releases. It consists of two pre-formed transparent plastic panels joined together, encasing the jewel boxed CD. Often, the booklet is removed from the jewel box and placed in the upper section of the bubble pack for display purposes.

BOOMERANG

SPUNKADELIC

LABEL
SBK
ART DIRECTION
JANET PERR
DESIGN
JANET PERR

THE DIGIPAK

The Digipak was the earliest innovation in packaging for promotional CD's. Created by AGI, Incorporated, a U.S. CD manufacturer. The Digipak includes a plastic holding piece for the CD, as well as one or more cardboard flaps, providing three or more panels available for printing.

TWISTED

KANE ROBERTS

LABEL
GEFFEN
PACKAGING
CONCEPT
SAMANTHA HART
ART DIRECTION
KEVIN REAGAN
DESIGN
KEVIN REAGAN
PHOTOGRAPHY
ROBERT JOHN
WAYNE MASER

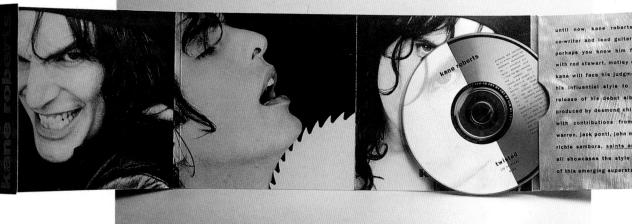

until now, kane roberts was best known as co-writer and lead guitarist for alice cooper or perhaps you know him from his collaborations with rod stewart, motley crue, and guns n' roses. kane will face his judgment day when he brings his influential style to the forefront with the release of his debut album saints and sinners. produced by desmond child and sir arthur payson with contributions from kane's friends diane warren, jack ponti, john mccurry, jon bon jovi, and richie sambora, saints and sinners once and for all showcases the style and intense personality of this emerging superstar.

THE SMART-PAK

The Smart-Pak was created by Samantha Hart (then Samantha Martinez) of Geffen Records, as a self-mailer promotional package. The Smart-Pak is made of recycled paperboard and contains only a small amount of discardable material. A flap containing the disc folds into one or more panels, and the flap section is removable, leaving a neat, clean storage pack.

"The package can be run in large quantities, thus lowering the per unit cost and then surprinting the specific artist/title identification as needed. In this way promotional mailings can be sent out quickly and with no obsolescence. Potential retail sales could result from mail-order situations that can be implemented in numerous ways of which I am currently exploring."

SAMANTHA HART, GEFFEN RECORDS

DISAPPEARER

SONIC YOUTH

LABEL

GEFFEN

PACKAGING
CONCEPT

SAMANTHA HART

ART DIRECTION

KEVIN REAGAN

DESIGN

KEVIN REAGAN

ILLUSTRATION

**RAYMOND
PETTIBONE**

THE DIGITRAK

Also a creation of AGI, the Digitrak satisfies the desire to keep disposable materials to a minimum while retaining the six-inch by twelve-inch package format that has been so successful in U.S. stores. This retail package design is now receiving some competition from other manufacturers of CD packaging. Two small disposable plastic *"tracks"* are removed and discarded, to fold the retail box into a gate-fold-style package. Still in limited use at this writing, the Digi-trak shows much promise for replacing the longbox in coming years.

THE SOUL CAGES
STING

LABEL
A&M
ART DIRECTION
RICH FRANKEL
LEN PELTIER
DESIGN
RICH FRANKEL
LEN PELTIER
PHOTOGRAPHY
GUZMAN
ILLUSTRATION
STEVEN CAMPBELL

*"The Digitrak started when Rich Frankel [of A&M] was work-
ing with AGI on new packaging. Sting had told us long before that
the longbox had to go, so his was the first CD to be released in this
environmentally-sound package."*

LEN PELTIER, A&M RECORDS

LUCK OF THE DRAW
BONNIE RAITT

LABEL
CAPITOL
ART DIRECTION
TOMMY STEELE
DESIGN
JEFFERY FEY
PHOTOGRAPHY
MERLYN ROSENBERG
LETTERING
MARGO CHASE

"Following up the release of the Sting CD, we wanted to use an environmental package for Bonnie Raitt's album. She's environmentally conscious and we felt that it was important to find an alternative remedy for the longbox that was politically and environmentally correct. Since the manufacturing for the Digitrak was already set up, we were ready to go and able to use recycled board."

TOMMY STEELE, CAPITOL RECORDS

LASERFILE

A product of
Reynard CVC Inc.,
the Laserfile package
is marketed with the
tag line, *"Packaging
designed with the planet
in mind."* Identical in
dimensions to the
jewel box, Laserfile
offers a retail option
that approximates
the shape of the
longbox. This retail
form includes a
retractable disc tray,
which limits discard-
able material to
shrink-wrapping.
Made from almost
100% recycled and
recyclable materials,
Laserfile accommo-
dates a standard size
booklet printed on
recycled paper, and
it allows the user to
feed a CD directly
into a car stereo CD
player without
removing it from the
disc tray.

ECO-PAK

The Eco-Pak is a future retail packaging item that proposes to replace the longbox. With only shrink-wrapping to discard, the Eco-Pak is environmentally sound, and collapses from the shape of the longbox to the dimensions of the jewel box. The manufacturer, Ivy Hill Corporation, describes this package as analagous to the record jacket, its folding panels and unique closure providing more opportunity for design and enjoyment.

SPECIAL RETAIL PACKAGING
Individualized packaging is most common among smaller labels and independent releases. Often the product of the recording artist rather than the label, these retail packages reflect the need among designers of promotional CD's to expand their creativity.

SLP
SLP

LABEL
SELEKTION
ART DIRECTION
CHARLY STEIGER
DESIGN
CHARLY STEIGER

The booklet was conceived and designed as an independent art object, separate from the recording. The use of transparent papers is derived from the materials used by the designer as fine art, rather than being used for the sheer sake of design. Printing the artwork on transparent paper puts a special accent on the different layers and their interchange.

JUST AN ILLUSION

ZOVIET-FRANCE

LABEL
STAALPLAAT

PACKAGING
CONCEPT
STAALPLAAT

DESIGN
BEN PONTON

ONE FOOT IN THE GRAVE

Z'EV

LABEL
TOUCH
ART DIRECTION
SIMON STAINES
TOUCH
DESIGN
SIMON STAINES
TOUCH
BOOKLET EDITOR
JON WOZENCROFT

The unique packaging for Hafler Trio releases was designed by the recording artist in keeping with the originality of the music.

INTOUTOF

THE HAFLER TRIO

LABEL
TOUCH
ART DIRECTION
A.M. McKENZIE
TOUCH
DESIGN
A.M. McKENZIE
TOUCH

'TOURIST WITH PENDULUM'

ULTRASONIC SETTING UP
PROCEDURE
ISLE OF DOGS
GAP IN THE POPE'S JAR
TRIBAL HOURGLASS GEOMETRY
THE QUEST FOR RIGEL 6
ANTHROPOLOGICAL G.I.G. FOR
ST. DAVID

'CHRONOS DESTROYED'
DO
EXPERIMENTAL EARTH PHYSICS
MINUS THE SEA AND THE SKY

DISLOCATION

THE HAFLER TRIO

LABEL
TOUCH
ART DIRECTION
A.M. McKENZIE
TOUCH
DESIGN
A.M. McKENZIE
TOUCH

IGNOTUM PER
IGNOTUS
THE HAFLER TRIO

LABEL
TOUCH
ART DIRECTION
A.M. McKENZIE
TOUCH
DESIGN
A.M. McKENZIE
TOUCH

THE CAPITOL YEARS

FRANK SINATRA

LABEL

CAPITOL

ART DIRECTION

TOMMY STEELE

DESIGN

ANDY ENGEL

SOUND + VISION
DAVID BOWIE

LABEL
RYKODISC
ART DIRECTION
**ROGER GORMAN &
ASSOCIATES/
REINER DESIGN
CONSULTANTS**
DESIGN
**ROGER GORMAN &
ASSOCIATES/
REINER DESIGN
CONSULTANTS**

One of the most riveting retail packages today, this had to be included in the Innovative Packaging section because of its ground-breaking and Grammy Award-winning design. The use of three distinct design layers working together accents the wholeness of the recording artist's material.

PLAY IT BY EAR

**THE FIRST CD
GAME**

LABEL

RYKODISC

DESIGN

**CHARLES R.
BRUNNER**

PLAY IT BY EAR introduces a new concept — a game played on a CD player. This package overcomes a number of design obstacles. It combines the compact and elegant style of CD packaging with the large and *"splashy"* style of game packaging. It also conveys that although the game is not a music product, record consumers would enjoy it. Finally, it approaches the fact that at a purchase price of $40, the game is not just for music buffs.

PHOTO COURTESY RYKODISC

FOLIO 1 is a collection of photographic images on CD ROM for use in graphic design. The graphics used in the design were created in Adobe Illustrator, and the final designs were placed into Quark Xpress for final layout and separations.

FOLIO 1

CD ROM

COMPANY
D'PIX
ART DIRECTION
JOHN GARRISON
DESIGN
JOHN GARRISON
TOD MOCK

RETAIL

Although new forms of pack-
aging can create limitless
design options, those related
to standard packaging
types are hardly restrictive.
Since the design focus has
shifted from LP albums to
CDs, designers and art
directors have expanded the
limitations of retail design
for music media.

TO BE
CONTINUED...
ELTON JOHN

LABEL
MCA
ART DIRECTION
DAVID COSTA
DAVID PALMER
FOR WHEREFORE
ART
DESIGN
DAVID COSTA
DAVID PALMER
FOR WHEREFORE
ART
COMPUTER IMAGING
SHEENA DUGGAL
SILK SCREENING
WAYNE JOHNSON
OF 1st CHOICE
SCREEN PRINT

ACHTUNG BABY

U2

LABEL

ISLAND

DESIGN

**STEVE AVERILL
AND SHAUGHN
MCGRATH**

**WORKS ASSOCI-
ATES (DUBLIN)**

PHOTOGRAPHY

ANTON CORBIJN

RITCHIE SMITH

ILLUSTRATION

CHARLIE WHISKER

LABEL

ISLAND

DESIGN

**STEVE AVERILL
AND SHAUGHN
MCGRATH**

**WORKS ASSOCI-
ATES (DUBLIN)**

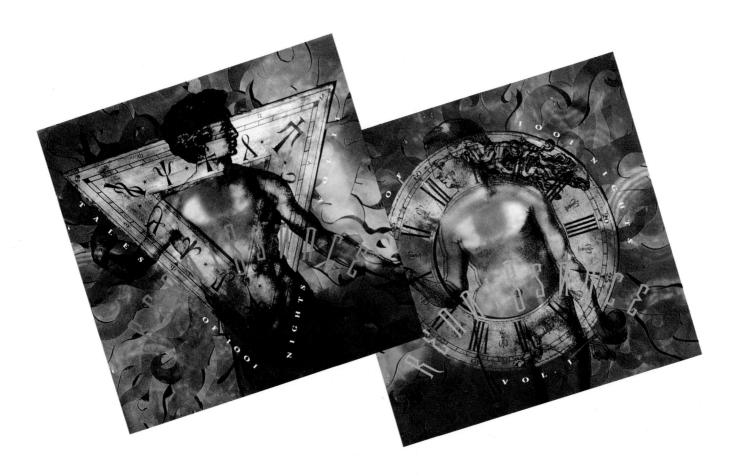

TALES OF 1001
NIGHTS
VOLUMES 1 & 2
RENAISSANCE

LABEL
SIRE
ART DIRECTION
MARGO CHASE
DESIGN
LORNA STOVALL
PHOTOGRAPHY
SIDNEY COOPER
MARGO CHASE

DIAMONDS AND PEARLS

PRINCE & THE NEW POWER GENERATION

LABEL

PAISLEY PARK/ WARNER BROTHERS

ART DIRECTION

JEFF GOLD

TOM RECCHION

DESIGN

GREG ROSS

HOLOGRAM

CHRIS MAHNE

SHARON McCORMACK

PETER SORBO

EYE LOGO

STEPHANIE BENNETT

PHOTOGRAPHY

JOEL LARSON

SAY AHH

MERCHANTS OF VENUS

LABEL

ELEKTRA

ART DIRECTION

MANHATTAN DESIGN

DESIGN

MANHATTAN DESIGN

PHOTOGRAPHY

MICHAEL LAVINE

SPACE PHOTOS

NASA

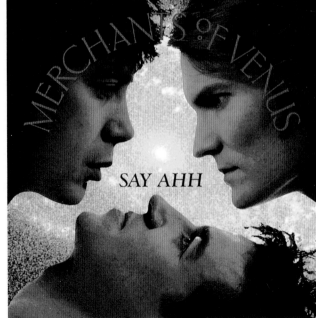

USE YOUR ILLUSION
I & II
GUNS N' ROSES

LABEL
GEFFEN
ART DIRECTION &
DESIGN
KEVIN REAGAN
SLASH
W. AXL ROSE
PRODUCTION
WENDY SHERMAN
COVER PAINTING
MARK KOSTABI

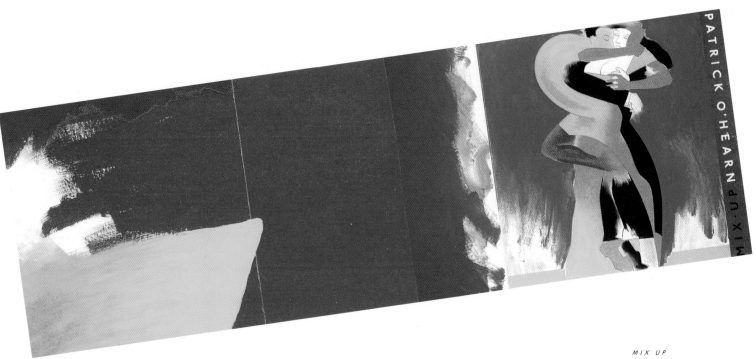

MIX UP
PATRICK O'HEARN

LABEL
PRIVATE MUSIC
ART DIRECTION
NORMAN MOORE
DESIGN
NORMAN MOORE
ARTWORK
ALLEN JONES

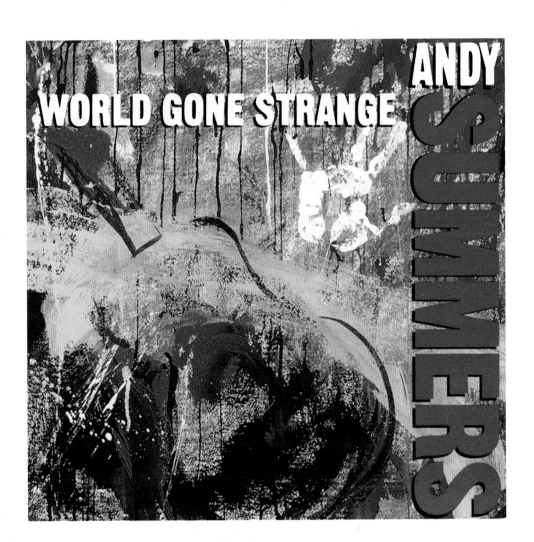

WORLD GONE
STRANGE
ANDY SUMMERS

LABEL
PRIVATE MUSIC
ART DIRECTION
NORMAN MOORE
DESIGN
NORMAN MOORE
PHOTOGRAPHY
**MERLYN
ROSENBERG**
COVER ART
ANDY SUMMERS

CHARMED LIFE
BILLY IDOL

LABEL
CHRYSALIS
ART DIRECTION
PETER CORRISTON
DESIGN
RANDALL MARTIN
PHOTOGRAPHY
**GEORGE KERRIG
AGUILERA-
HELLWEG**

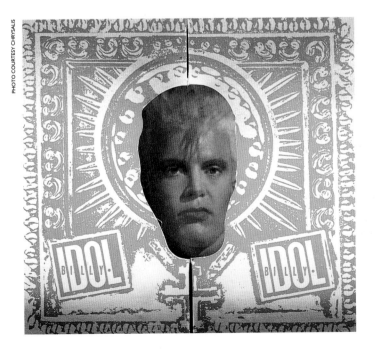

A special collector's edition CD was released to accompany the latest Billy Idol CD. Intricate die-cutting in both the longbox and CD cover enhance the multi-dimensionality of the design. The package was intended to emulate a small shrine, playing off the artist's name.

CHUCK BERRY

CHUCK BERRY

LABEL

MCA

ART DIRECTION

VARTAN

DESIGN

**DZN, THE DESIGN
GROUP**

PHOTOGRAPHY

**COURTESY OF
SHOWTIME
ARCHIVES
(TORONTO)
ARCHIVE/ESCOTT**

MUDDY WATERS

MUDDY WATERS

LABEL

MCA

ART DIRECTION

VARTAN

DESIGN

**DZN, THE DESIGN
GROUP**

PHOTOGRAPHY

**DON BRONSTEIN,
COURTSEY OF THE
BLUES ARCHIVE,
UNIVERSITY OF
MISSISSIPPI**

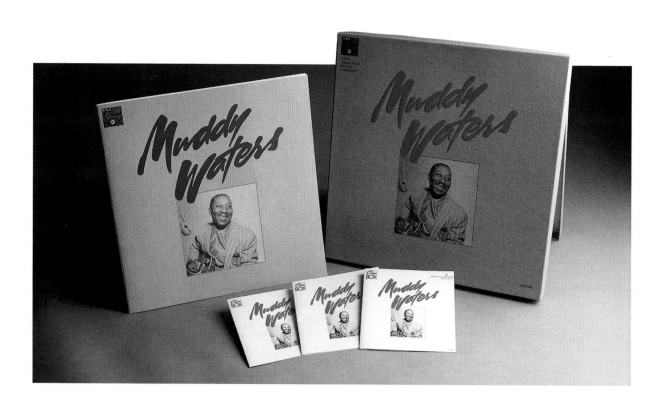

BO DIDDLEY

BO DIDDLEY

LABEL

MCA

ART DIRECTION

VARTAN

DESIGN

DZN, THE DESIGN GROUP

PHOTOGRAPHY

COURTESY OF SHOWTIME ARCHIVES (TORONTO)

RIVERS GONNA RISE
PATRICK O'HEARN

LABEL
PRIVATE MUSIC
ART DIRECTION
NORMAN MOORE
DESIGN
NORMAN MOORE
PHOTOGRAPHY
ROBERT TORBET

INDIGO
PATRICK O'HEARN

LABEL
PRIVATE MUSIC
ART DIRECTION
NORMAN MOORE
DESIGN
NORMAN MOORE
PHOTOGRAPHY
DOUGLAS BROTHERS

*WITOLD
LUTOSLAWSKI*

KRONOS QUARTET

LABEL

ELEKTRA

ART DIRECTION

FRANK OLINSKY

PAT GORMAN

**MANHATTAN
DESIGN**

DESIGN

FRANK OLINSKY

PAT GORMAN

PHOTOGRAPHY

ADAM FUSS

BLACK ANGELS

KRONOS QUARTET

LABEL

ELEKTRA

ART DIRECTION

FRANK OLINSKY

PAT GORMAN

**MANHATTAN
DESIGN**

DESIGN

FRANK OLINSKY

PAT GORMAN

**MANHATTAN
DESIGN**

ILLUSTRATION

MATT MAHURIN

ASTOR PIAZZOLLA

KRONOS QUARTET

LABEL

ELEKTRA

ART DIRECTION

FRANK OLINSKY

PAT GORMAN

**MANHATTAN
DESIGN**

DESIGN

FRANK OLINSKY

PAT GORMAN

**MANHATTAN
DESIGN**

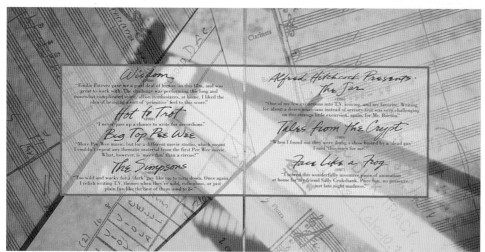

FILM & TELEVISION
MUSIC VOLUME ONE

DANNY ELFMAN

LABEL
MCA

ART DIRECTION
VARTAN

DESIGN
LARRY
BROOKS/KOSH
BROOKS DESIGN

PHOTOGRAPHY
DENNIS KEELEY

DAVID NORWOOD

STUART WATSON

SONGS FOR DRELLA
LOU REED/ JOHN
CALE

LABEL
WARNER
BROS./SIRE

ART DIRECTION &
DESIGN
TOM RECCHION

SYLVIA REED

PHOTO OF ANDY
WARHOL
BILLY NAME

PHOTO OF LOU
REED/ JOHN CALE
JAMES HAMILTON

PERFORMANCE
PHOTOS
JEROME SIRLIN,
RISE'

THE LEGEND AND THE LEGACY

LES PAUL

LABEL

CAPITOL

ART DIRECTION

TOMMY STEELE

JEFFERY FEY

DESIGN

JEFFERY FEY

PETER GRANT

BOOK DESIGN

PETER GRANT

PHOTO RESEARCH FOR CAPITOL RECORDS ARCHIVE

BRAD BENEDICT

COVER PHOTOGRAPHY, COLOR COLLAGE PHOTOS

LARRY DuPONT

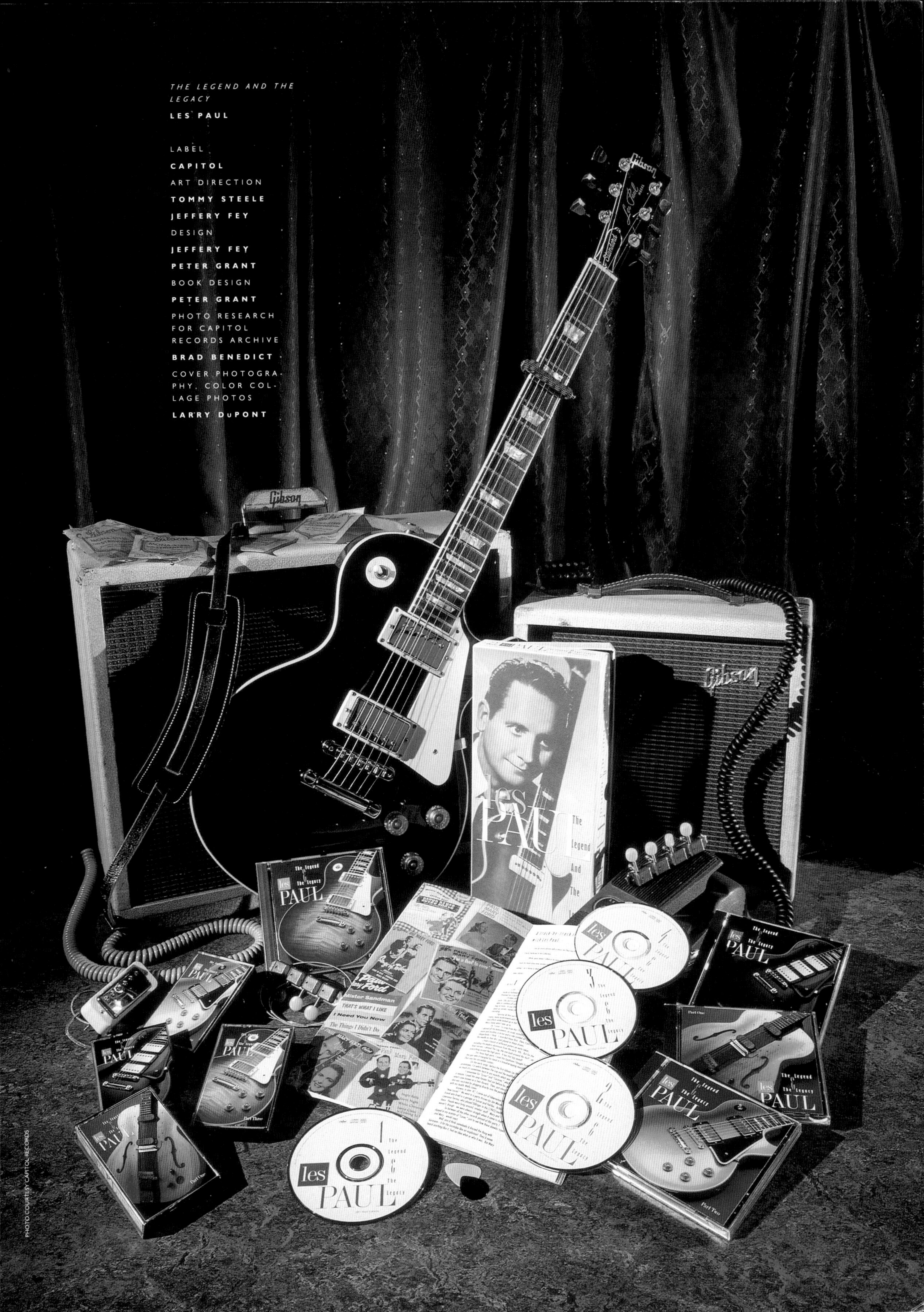

PHOTO COURTESY CAPITOL RECORDS

GREEN

R.E.M.

LABEL
WARNER BROTHERS
ART DIRECTION
**FRANK OLINSKY/
MANHATTAN
DESIGN**
JON McCAFFERTY
J.M. STIPE
DESIGN
**FRANK OLINSKY/
MANHATTAN
DESIGN**
JON McCAFFERTY
J.M. STIPE
PHOTOGRAPHY
JEM COHEN
JON McCAFFERTY
J.M. STIPE
MICHAEL TIGHE

The original title of
the album was
G4EEN (a typo-
graphic error that
the bandleader
liked), which was
echoed in the use of
the number 4 printed
in a spot varnish.
The Dadaist idea of
an album entitled
Green with no green
coloring in it com-
bined with ecologi-
cal images of trees
and leaves makes a
complete package
that fits in well with
the anti-radio orien-
tation of the band.

*THESE PEOPLE ARE
NUTS*

VARIOUS ARTISTS

LABEL
IRS

ART DIRECTION
HUGH BROWN

DESIGN
HUGH BROWN

PHOTOGRAPHY
HUGH BROWN

PHOTO COURTESY CAPITOL RECORDS

FEELS GOOD

TONY TONI TONÉ

LABEL
POLYGRAM
ART DIRECTION
MICHAEL BAYS
ALLI TRUCH
DESIGN
MICHAEL BAYS
ALLI TRUCH

THE MILLION DOLLAR QUARTET
ELVIS PRESLEY

LABEL
BMG/RCA
ART DIRECTION
NORMAN MOORE
DESIGN
NORMAN MOORE
PHOTOGRAPHY
COURTESY MARION KEISKER

THE "LOST" ALBUM
ELVIS PRESLEY

LABEL
RCA
ART DIRECTION
NORMAN MOORE
DESIGN
NORMAN MOORE
PHOTOGRAPHY
PHILLIP SALTONSTALL

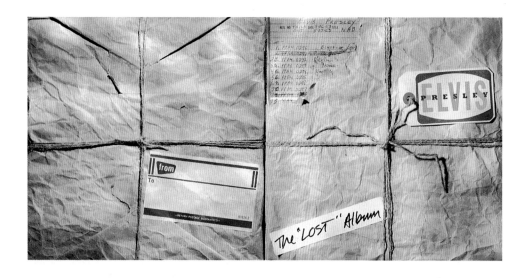

RUBAIYAT

VARIOUS ARTISTS

LABEL
ELEKTRA
ART DIRECTION
**PAT GORMAN
FRANK OLINSKY
MANHATTAN
DESIGN**
DESIGN
**PAT GORMAN
FRANK OLINSKY
MANHATTAN
DESIGN**
PHOTOGRAPHY
**DOUG & MIKE
STARN**

NEVERLAND
SUZANNE CIANI

LABEL
PRIVATE MUSIC
ART DIRECTION
CAREN J. MARTINEAU CREATIVE
DESIGN
CAREN J. MARTINEAU CREATIVE
PHOTOGRAPHY
CHRIS CALLIS
PHOTO TINTING
SHERI COHEN

PIANISSIMO
SUZANNE CIANI

LABEL
PRIVATE MUSIC
ART DIRECTION
MELANIE PENNY
DESIGN
MARGO CHASE
PHOTOGRAPHY
DIANE RUBINGER
PHOTO ILLUSTRATION
ROBBIE CAVOLINA

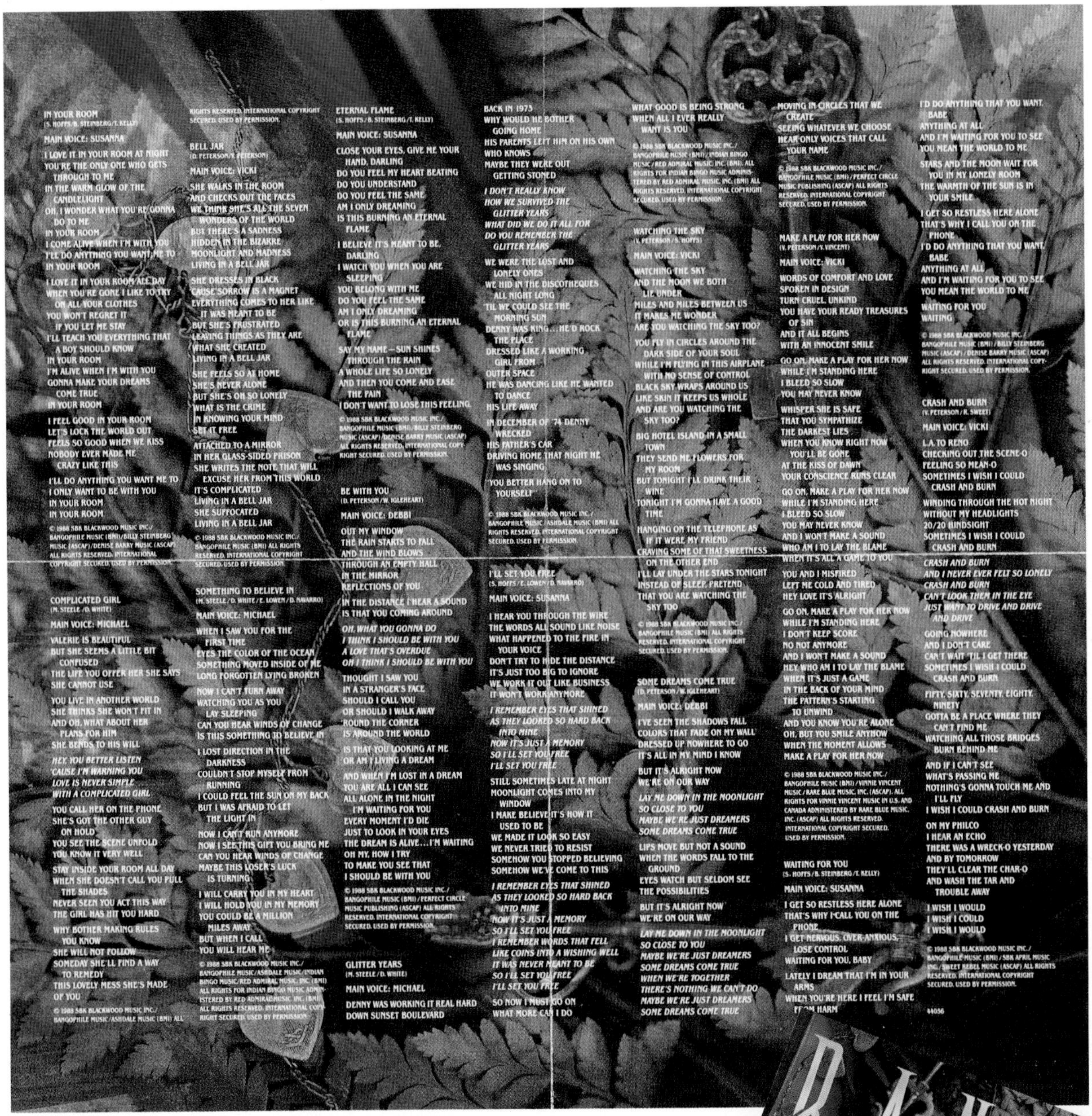

IN YOUR ROOM
(S. HOFFS/B. STEINBERG/T. KELLY)

MAIN VOICE: SUSANNA

I LOVE IT IN YOUR ROOM AT NIGHT
YOU'RE THE ONLY ONE WHO GETS
   THROUGH TO ME
IN THE WARM GLOW OF THE
   CANDLELIGHT
OH, I WONDER WHAT YOU'RE GONNA
   DO TO ME
IN YOUR ROOM
I COME ALIVE WHEN I'M WITH YOU
I'LL DO ANYTHING YOU WANT ME TO
IN YOUR ROOM
I LOVE IT IN YOUR ROOM ALL DAY
WHEN YOU'RE GONE I LIKE TO TRY
   ON ALL YOUR CLOTHES
YOU WON'T REGRET IT
IF YOU LET ME STAY
I'LL TEACH YOU EVERYTHING THAT
   A BOY SHOULD KNOW
IN YOUR ROOM
I'M ALIVE WHEN I'M WITH YOU
GONNA MAKE YOUR DREAMS
   COME TRUE
IN YOUR ROOM
I FEEL GOOD IN YOUR ROOM
LET'S LOCK THE WORLD OUT
FEELS SO GOOD WHEN WE KISS
NOBODY EVER MADE ME
   CRAZY LIKE THIS
I'LL DO ANYTHING YOU WANT ME TO
I ONLY WANT TO BE WITH YOU
IN YOUR ROOM
IN YOUR ROOM

© 1988 BLACKWOOD MUSIC INC./
BANGOPHILE MUSIC (BMI)/BILLY STEINBERG
MUSIC (ASCAP)/DENISE BARRY MUSIC (ASCAP)
ALL RIGHTS RESERVED. INTERNATIONAL
COPYRIGHT SECURED. USED BY PERMISSION

COMPLICATED GIRL
(M. STEELE/D. WHITE)

MAIN VOICE: MICHAEL

VALERIE IS BEAUTIFUL
BUT SHE SEEMS A LITTLE BIT
   CONFUSED
THE LIFE YOU OFFER HER SHE SAYS
SHE CANNOT USE
YOU LIVE IN ANOTHER WORLD
SHE THINKS SHE WON'T FIT IN
AND OH, WHAT ABOUT HER
   PLANS FOR HIM
SHE BENDS TO HIS WILL
HEY YOU BETTER LISTEN
'CAUSE I'M WARNING YOU
LOVE IS NEVER SIMPLE
WITH A COMPLICATED GIRL
YOU CALL HER ON THE PHONE
SHE'S GOT THE OTHER GUY
   ON HOLD
YOU SEE THE SCENE UNFOLD
YOU KNOW IT VERY WELL
STAY INSIDE YOUR ROOM ALL DAY
WHEN SHE DOESN'T CALL YOU PULL
   THE SHADES
NEVER SEEN YOU ACT THIS WAY
THE GIRL HAS HIT YOU HARD
WHY BOTHER MAKING RULES
   YOU KNOW
SHE WILL NOT FOLLOW
SOMEDAY SHE'LL FIND A WAY
   TO REMEDY
THIS LOVELY MESS SHE'S MADE
   OF YOU

© 1988 SBK BLACKWOOD MUSIC INC./
BANGOPHILE MUSIC/ASBDALE MUSIC (BMI) ALL
RIGHTS RESERVED. INTERNATIONAL COPY-
RIGHT SECURED. USED BY PERMISSION

RIGHTS RESERVED. INTERNATIONAL COPYRIGHT
SECURED. USED BY PERMISSION.

BELL JAR
(D. PETERSON/V. PETERSON)

MAIN VOICE: VICKI

SHE WALKS IN THE ROOM
AND CHECKS OUT THE FACES
WE THINK SHE'S ALL THE SEVEN
   WONDERS OF THE WORLD
BUT THERE'S A SADNESS
HIDDEN IN THE BIZARRE
MOONLIGHT AND MADNESS
LIVING IN A BELL JAR
SHE DRESSES IN BLACK
'CAUSE SORROW IS A MAGNET
EVERYTHING COMES TO HER LIKE
   IT WAS MEANT TO BE
BUT SHE'S FRUSTRATED
LEAVING THINGS AS THEY ARE
WHAT SHE CREATED
LIVING IN A BELL JAR
SHE FEELS SO AT HOME
SHE'S NEVER ALONE
BUT SHE'S OH SO LONELY
WHAT IS THE CRIME
IN KNOWING YOUR MIND
SET IT FREE
ATTACHED TO A MIRROR
IN HER GLASS-SIDED PRISON
SHE WRITES THE NOTE THAT WILL
   EXCUSE HER FROM THIS WORLD
IT'S COMPLICATED
LIVING IN A BELL JAR
SHE SUFFOCATED
LIVING IN A BELL JAR

© 1988 SBK BLACKWOOD MUSIC INC./
BANGOPHILE MUSIC (BMI) ALL RIGHTS
RESERVED. INTERNATIONAL COPYRIGHT
SECURED. USED BY PERMISSION

SOMETHING TO BELIEVE IN
(M. STEELE/D. WHITE/E. LOWEN/D. NAVARRO)

MAIN VOICE: MICHAEL

WHEN I SAW YOU FOR THE
   FIRST TIME
EYES THE COLOR OF THE OCEAN
SOMETHING MOVED INSIDE OF ME
LONG FORGOTTEN LYING BROKEN
NOW I CAN'T TURN AWAY
WATCHING YOU AS YOU
   LAY SLEEPING
CAN YOU HEAR WINDS OF CHANGE
IS THIS SOMETHING TO BELIEVE IN
I LOST DIRECTION IN THE
   DARKNESS
COULDN'T STOP MYSELF FROM
   RUNNING
I COULD FEEL THE SUN ON MY BACK
BUT I WAS AFRAID TO LET
   THE LIGHT IN
NOW I CAN'T RUN ANYMORE
NOW I SEE THIS GIFT YOU BRING ME
CAN YOU HEAR WINDS OF CHANGE
MAYBE THIS LOSER'S LUCK
   IS TURNING
I WILL CARRY YOU IN MY HEART
I WILL HOLD YOU IN MY MEMORY
MILES AWAY
BUT WHEN I CALL
YOU WILL HEAR ME

© 1988 SBK BLACKWOOD MUSIC INC./
BANGOPHILE MUSIC (BMI)/PERFECT CIRCLE
MUSIC PUBLISHING (ASCAP) ALL RIGHTS
RESERVED. INTERNATIONAL COPYRIGHT
SECURED. USED BY PERMISSION.

GLITTER YEARS
(M. STEELE/D. WHITE)

MAIN VOICE: MICHAEL

DENNY WAS WORKING IT REAL HARD
DOWN SUNSET BOULEVARD

ETERNAL FLAME
(S. HOFFS/B. STEINBERG/T. KELLY)

MAIN VOICE: SUSANNA

CLOSE YOUR EYES, GIVE ME YOUR
   HAND, DARLING
DO YOU FEEL MY HEART BEATING
DO YOU UNDERSTAND
DO YOU FEEL THE SAME
AM I ONLY DREAMING
IS THIS BURNING AN ETERNAL
   FLAME
I BELIEVE IT'S MEANT TO BE,
   DARLING
I WATCH YOU WHEN YOU ARE
   SLEEPING
YOU BELONG WITH ME
DO YOU FEEL THE SAME
AM I ONLY DREAMING
OR IS THIS BURNING AN ETERNAL
   FLAME
SAY MY NAME – SUN SHINES
   THROUGH THE RAIN
A WHOLE LIFE SO LONELY
AND THEN YOU COME AND EASE
   THE PAIN
I DON'T WANT TO LOSE THIS FEELING.

© 1988 SBK BLACKWOOD MUSIC INC./
BANGOPHILE MUSIC/BILLY STEINBERG
MUSIC (ASCAP)/DENISE BARRY MUSIC (ASCAP)
ALL RIGHTS RESERVED. INTERNATIONAL COPY-
RIGHT SECURED. USED BY PERMISSION.

BE WITH YOU
(D. PETERSON/W. IGLEHEART)

MAIN VOICE: DEBBI

OUT MY WINDOW
THE RAIN STARTS TO FALL
AND THE WIND BLOWS
THROUGH AN EMPTY HALL
IN THE MIRROR
REFLECTIONS OF YOU
IN THE DISTANCE I HEAR A SOUND
IS THAT YOU COMING AROUND
OH, WHAT YOU GONNA DO
I THINK I SHOULD BE WITH YOU
A LOVE THAT'S OVERDUE
OH I THINK I SHOULD BE WITH YOU
THOUGHT I SAW YOU
IN A STRANGER'S FACE
SHOULD I CALL YOU
OR SHOULD I WALK AWAY
ROUND THE CORNER
IS AROUND THE WORLD
IS THAT YOU LOOKING AT ME
OR AM I LIVING A DREAM
AND WHEN I'M LOST IN A DREAM
YOU ARE ALL I CAN SEE
ALL ALONE IN THE NIGHT
I'M WAITING FOR YOU
EVERY MOMENT I'D DIE
JUST TO LOOK IN YOUR EYES
THE DREAM IS ALIVE…I'M WAITING
OH MY, HOW I TRY
TO MAKE YOU SEE THAT
I SHOULD BE WITH YOU

© 1988 SBK BLACKWOOD MUSIC INC./
BANGOPHILE MUSIC/ASBDALE MUSIC (INDIAN
BINGO MUSIC)/RED ADMIRAL MUSIC, INC. (BMI)
ALL RIGHTS FOR INDIAN BINGO MUSIC ADMIN-
ISTERED BY RED ADMIRAL MUSIC, INC. (BMI)
ALL RIGHTS RESERVED. INTERNATIONAL COPY-
RIGHT SECURED. USED BY PERMISSION

BACK IN 1973
WHY WOULD HE BOTHER
   GOING HOME
HIS PARENTS LEFT HIM ON HIS OWN
   WHO KNOWS
MAYBE THEY WERE OUT
   GETTING STONED
I DON'T REALLY KNOW
HOW WE SURVIVED THE
   GLITTER YEARS
WHAT DID WE DO IT ALL FOR
DO YOU REMEMBER THE
   GLITTER YEARS
WE WERE THE LOST AND
   LONELY ONES
WE HID IN THE DISCOTHEQUES
   ALL NIGHT LONG
TIL WE COULD SEE THE
   MORNING SUN
DENNY WAS KING…HE'D ROCK
   THE PLACE
DRESSED LIKE A WORKING
   GIRL FROM
OUTER SPACE
HE WAS DANCING LIKE HE WANTED
   TO DANCE
HIS LIFE AWAY
IN DECEMBER OF '74 DENNY
WRECKED
HIS FATHER'S CAR
DRIVING HOME THAT NIGHT HE
   WAS SINGING
YOU BETTER HANG ON TO
   YOURSELF

© 1988 SBK BLACKWOOD MUSIC INC./
BANGOPHILE MUSIC/ASBDALE MUSIC (BMI) ALL
RIGHTS RESERVED. INTERNATIONAL COPYRIGHT
SECURED. USED BY PERMISSION.

I'LL SET YOU FREE
(S. HOFFS/E. LOWEN/D. NAVARRO)

MAIN VOICE: SUSANNA

I HEAR YOU THROUGH THE WIRE
THE WORDS ALL SOUND LIKE NOISE
WHAT HAPPENED TO THE FIRE IN
   YOUR VOICE
DON'T TRY TO HIDE THE DISTANCE
IT'S JUST TOO BIG TO IGNORE
WE WORK IT OUT LIKE BUSINESS
IT WON'T WORK ANYMORE
I REMEMBER EYES THAT SHINED
AS THEY LOOKED SO HARD BACK
   INTO MINE
NOW IT'S JUST A MEMORY
SO I'LL SET YOU FREE
I'LL SET YOU FREE
STILL SOMETIMES LATE AT NIGHT
MOONLIGHT COMES INTO MY
   WINDOW
I MAKE BELIEVE IT'S HOW IT
   USED TO BE
WE MADE IT LOOK SO EASY
WE NEVER TRIED TO RESIST
SOMEHOW YOU STOPPED BELIEVING
SOMEHOW WE'VE COME TO THIS
I REMEMBER EYES THAT SHINED
AS THEY LOOKED SO HARD BACK
   INTO MINE
NOW IT'S JUST A MEMORY
SO I'LL SET YOU FREE
I REMEMBER WORDS THAT FELL
LIKE COINS INTO A WISHING WELL
IT WAS NEVER MEANT TO BE
SO I'LL SET YOU FREE
I'LL SET YOU FREE
SO NOW I MUST GO ON
WHAT MORE CAN I DO

WHAT GOOD IS BEING STRONG
WHEN ALL I EVER REALLY
   WANT IS YOU

© 1988 SBK BLACKWOOD MUSIC INC./
BANGOPHILE MUSIC (BMI)/INDIAN BINGO
MUSIC/ASBDALE MUSIC, INC. (BMI) ALL RIGHTS
FOR INDIAN BINGO MUSIC ADMINIS-
TERED BY RED ADMIRAL MUSIC, INC. (BMI) ALL
RIGHTS RESERVED. INTERNATIONAL COPYRIGHT
SECURED. USED BY PERMISSION.

WATCHING THE SKY
(V. PETERSON/S. HOFFS)

MAIN VOICE: VICKI

WATCHING THE SKY
AND THE MOON WE BOTH
   LIE UNDER
MILES AND MILES BETWEEN US
IT MAKES ME WONDER
ARE YOU WATCHING THE SKY TOO?
YOU FLY IN CIRCLES AROUND THE
   DARK SIDE OF YOUR SOUL
WHILE I'M FLYING IN THIS AIRPLANE
   WITH NO SENSE OF CONTROL
BLACK SKY WRAPS AROUND US
LIKE SKIN IT KEEPS US WHOLE
AND ARE YOU WATCHING THE
   SKY TOO?
BIG HOTEL ISLAND IN A SMALL
   TOWN
THEY SEND ME FLOWERS FOR
   MY ROOM
BUT TONIGHT I'LL DRINK THEIR
   WINE
TONIGHT I'M GONNA HAVE A GOOD
   TIME
HANGING ON THE TELEPHONE AS
   IF IT WERE MY FRIEND
CRAVING SOME OF THAT SWEETNESS
   ON THE OTHER END
I'LL LAY UNDER THE STARS TONIGHT
INSTEAD OF SLEEP, PRETEND
THAT YOU ARE WATCHING THE
   SKY TOO

© 1988 SBK BLACKWOOD MUSIC INC./
BANGOPHILE MUSIC (BMI) ALL
RIGHTS RESERVED. INTERNATIONAL COPYRIGHT
SECURED. USED BY PERMISSION.

SOME DREAMS COME TRUE
(D. PETERSON/W. IGLEHEART)

MAIN VOICE: DEBBI

I'VE SEEN THE SHADOWS FALL
COLORS THAT FADE ON MY WALL
DRESSED UP NOWHERE TO GO
IT'S ALL IN MY MIND I KNOW
BUT IT'S ALRIGHT NOW
WE'RE ON OUR WAY
LAY ME DOWN IN THE MOONLIGHT
SO CLOSE TO YOU
MAYBE WE'RE JUST DREAMERS
SOME DREAMS COME TRUE
LIPS MOVE BUT NOT A SOUND
WHEN THE WORDS FALL TO THE
   GROUND
EYES WATCH BUT SELDOM SEE
THE POSSIBILITIES
BUT IT'S ALRIGHT NOW
WE'RE ON OUR WAY
LAY ME DOWN IN THE MOONLIGHT
SO CLOSE TO YOU
MAYBE WE'RE JUST DREAMERS
SOME DREAMS COME TRUE
WHEN WE'RE TOGETHER
THERE'S NOTHING WE CAN'T DO
MAYBE WE'RE JUST DREAMERS
SOME DREAMS COME TRUE

MOVING IN CIRCLES THAT WE
   CREATE
SEEING WHATEVER WE CHOOSE
HEAR ONLY VOICES THAT CALL
   YOUR NAME

© 1988 SBK BLACKWOOD MUSIC INC./
BANGOPHILE MUSIC (BMI)/PERFECT CIRCLE
MUSIC PUBLISHING (ASCAP) ALL RIGHTS
RESERVED. INTERNATIONAL COPYRIGHT
SECURED. USED BY PERMISSION.

MAKE A PLAY FOR HER NOW
(V. PETERSON/V. VINCENT)

MAIN VOICE: VICKI

WORDS OF COMFORT AND LOVE
SPOKEN IN DESIGN
TURN CRUEL, UNKIND
YOU HIDE YOUR READY TREASURES
   OF SIN
AND IT ALL BEGINS
WITH AN INNOCENT SMILE
GO ON, MAKE A PLAY FOR HER NOW
WHILE I'M STANDING HERE
I BLEED SO SLOW
YOU MAY NEVER KNOW
WHISPER SHE IS SAFE
THAT YOU SYMPATHIZE
THE DARKEST LIES
WHEN YOU KNOW RIGHT NOW
   YOU'LL BE GONE
AT THE KISS OF DAWN
YOUR CONSCIENCE RUNS CLEAR
GO ON, MAKE A PLAY FOR HER NOW
WHILE I'M STANDING HERE
I BLEED SO SLOW
YOU MAY NEVER KNOW
AND I WON'T MAKE A SOUND
WHO AM I TO LAY THE BLAME
WHEN IT'S ALL A GAME TO YOU
YOU AND I MISFIRED
LEFT ME COLD AND TIRED
HEY LOVE IT'S ALRIGHT
GO ON, MAKE A PLAY FOR HER NOW
WHILE I'M STANDING HERE
I DON'T KEEP SCORE
NO NOT ANYMORE
AND I WON'T MAKE A SOUND
HEY WHO AM I TO LAY THE BLAME
WHEN IT'S JUST A GAME
THE PATTERN'S STARTING
   TO UNWIND
AND YOU KNOW YOU'RE ALONE
OH, BUT YOU SMILE ANYHOW
WHEN THE MOMENT ALLOWS
MAKE A PLAY FOR HER NOW

WAITING FOR YOU
(S. HOFFS/B. STEINBERG/T. KELLY)

MAIN VOICE: SUSANNA

I GET SO RESTLESS HERE ALONE
THAT'S WHY I CALL YOU ON THE
   PHONE
I GET NERVOUS, OVER-ANXIOUS,
   LOSE CONTROL
WAITING FOR YOU, BABY
LATELY I DREAM THAT I'M IN YOUR
   ARMS
WHEN YOU'RE HERE I FEEL I'M SAFE
   FROM HARM

I'D DO ANYTHING THAT YOU WANT,
   BABE
ANYTHING AT ALL
AND I'M WAITING FOR YOU TO SEE
YOU MEAN THE WORLD TO ME
STARS AND THE MOON WAIT FOR
   YOU IN MY LONELY ROOM
THE WARMTH OF THE SUN IS IN
   YOUR SMILE
I GET SO RESTLESS HERE ALONE
THAT'S WHY I CALL YOU ON THE
   PHONE
I'D DO ANYTHING THAT YOU WANT,
   BABE
ANYTHING AT ALL
AND I'M WAITING FOR YOU TO SEE
YOU MEAN THE WORLD TO ME
WAITING FOR YOU
WAITING

© 1988 SBK BLACKWOOD MUSIC INC./
BANGOPHILE MUSIC (BMI) BILLY STEINBERG
MUSIC (ASCAP)/DENISE BARRY MUSIC (ASCAP)
ALL RIGHTS RESERVED. INTERNATIONAL COPY-
RIGHT SECURED. USED BY PERMISSION.

CRASH AND BURN
(V. PETERSON/R. SWEET)

MAIN VOICE: VICKI

L.A TO RENO
CHECKING OUT THE SCENE-O
FEELING SO MEAN-O
SOMETIMES I WISH I COULD
   CRASH AND BURN
WINDING THROUGH THE HOT NIGHT
WITHOUT MY HEADLIGHTS
20/20 HINDSIGHT
SOMETIMES I WISH I COULD
   CRASH AND BURN
CRASH AND BURN
AND I NEVER EVER FELT SO LONELY
CRASH AND BURN
CAN'T LOOK THEM IN THE EYE
JUST WANT TO DRIVE AND DRIVE
   AND DRIVE
GOING NOWHERE
AND I DON'T CARE
CAN'T WAIT 'TIL I GET THERE
SOMETIMES I WISH I COULD
   CRASH AND BURN
FIFTY, SIXTY, SEVENTY, EIGHTY,
   NINETY
GOTTA BE A PLACE WHERE THEY
   CAN'T FIND ME
WATCHING ALL THOSE BRIDGES
   BURN BEHIND ME
AND IF I CAN'T SEE
WHAT'S PASSING ME
NOTHING'S GONNA TOUCH ME AND
   I'LL FLY
I WISH I COULD CRASH AND BURN
ON MY PHILCO
I HEAR AN ECHO
THERE WAS A WRECK-O YESTERDAY
AND BY TOMORROW
THEY'LL CLEAR THE CHAR-O
AND WASH THE TAR AND
   TROUBLE AWAY
I WISH I WOULD
I WISH I WOULD
I WISH I WOULD

© 1988 SBK BLACKWOOD MUSIC INC./
BANGOPHILE MUSIC (BMI) / SBK APRIL MUSIC
INC./ SWEET REBEL MUSIC (ASCAP) ALL RIGHTS
RESERVED. INTERNATIONAL COPYRIGHT
SECURED. USED BY PERMISSION.

44056

EVERYTHING

BANGLES

LABEL

CBS

ART DIRECTION

TONY LANE

NANCY DONALD

LOGO DESIGN

DAVID COLEMAN

PHOTOGRAPHY

SHEILA ROCK

ART

**LESLEY SCHIFF,
COURTESY CANNON
U.S.A.**

LIFELINES-THE JIMI HENDRIX STORY

JIMI HENDRIX

LABEL
WARNER BROTHERS
ART DIRECTION
DEBORAH NORCROSS
DESIGN
DEBORAH NORCROSS
COVER PHOTOGRAPHY
MIKE POLILLO
COLORIZATION OF COVER PHOTO
KATHLEEN HESSION

NELSON RIDDLE, BEGINNING TO REACH
FAME FOR HIS WORK WITH FRANK
SINATRA AND NAT KING COLE, HAD
BEEN ONE OF THE ARRANGERS FOR "A
STAR IS BORN." IN MARCH, 1956, HE
WORKED ON HIS FIRST ALBUM WITH
JUDY, CALLED, SIMPLY "JUDY." A
YEAR LATER, SEVERAL SONGS AND
ARRANGEMENTS FROM THOSE SESSIONS
SERVED AS THE BASIS OF A 30-
MINUTE TV SPECIAL, "THE JUDY
GARLAND SHOW," WITH RIDDLE AS
CONDUCTOR. THE ALBUM WAS

...SCREEN. JUDY PERFORMED
...ED WITH THE GREAT
...BEEN SUGGESTED
...SON'S DRAMATIC
...E CERTAINLY

...APRIL
...1921
...CA...

THE ONE & ONLY
JUDY GARLAND

LABEL
CAPITOL
ART DIRECTION
TOMMY STEELE
DESIGN
VAN HAAFTEN
PHOTO RESEARCH
BRAD BENEDICT

INTO THE GREAT WIDE OPEN

TOM PETTY & THE HEARTBREAKERS

LABEL

MCA

ART DIRECTION

TINY BOUCHET & AWEST/BRASS RING CIRCUS STUDIOS

DESIGN COORDINATION

DZN, THE DESIGN GROUP

ILLUSTRATIONS

AWEST, KALYNN CAMBELL & BRASS RING STUDIOS

COVER ART

JOHN MATULKA

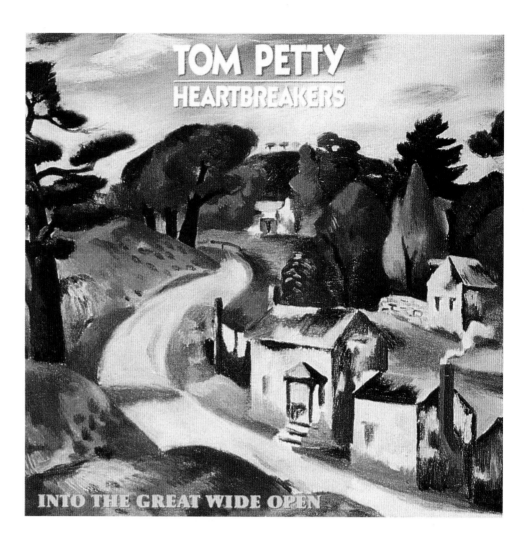

ELDORADO

PATRICK O'HEARN

LABEL

PRIVATE MUSIC

ART DIRECTION

NORMAN MOORE

DESIGN

NORMAN MOORE

PHOTOGRAPHY

MICHAEL MILLER

ILLUSTRATION

NANCY NIMOY

*THE CARL STALLING
PROJECT*

**THE CARL
STALLING PROJECT**

LABEL
WARNER
ART DIRECTION
TOM RECCHION
DESIGN
TOM RECCHION

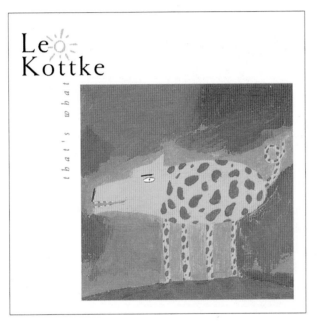

THAT'S WHAT
LEO KOTTKE

LABEL
PRIVATE MUSIC
ART DIRECTION
MELANIE PENNY
DESIGN
MIKE FINK
ARTWORK
LAURA LEVINE
PHOTOGRAPHY
TOM BERTHIAUME

MONSTER
FETCHIN' BONES

LABEL
CAPITOL
ART DIRECTION
TOMMY STEELE
DESIGN
PETER WALBERG
PHOTOGRAPHY
**JAY DAVID
BUCHSBAUM**
ARTWORK
MARK RYDEN

CATFISH RISING

JETHRO TULL

LABEL

CHRYSALIS

ART DIRECTION

**PHIL ROGERS &
JOHN PASCHE**

DESIGN

**PHIL ROGERS &
JOHN PASCHE**

ILLUSTRATION

JIM GIBSON

LOGO AND MONO-
GRAM

GEOFF HALPIN

THIS IS NOT LOVE

JETHRO TULL

LABEL

CHRYSALIS

ART DIRECTION

RANDALL MARTIN

DESIGN

RANDALL MARTIN

LOGO AND MONO-
GRAM

GEOFF HALPIN

ILLUSTRATION

JIM GIBSON

ALBUM DESIGN

**PHIL ROGERS
JOHN PASCHE**

PHOTO COURTESY CHRYSALIS

Shown here are the
album and single.
The single features a
time line foldout,
which was also used
as a promotional
piece.

Led Zeppelin

LED ZEPPELIN

LABEL
ATLANTIC
DESIGN
LARRY FREEMANTLE
ILLUSTRATION
MISSION CONTROL
IMAGING AND PHOTOGRAPHY
CHRIS WROE
JENNY MOORE

UNION
YES

LABEL
ARISTA
ART DIRECTION
CAROLYN QUAN
DESIGN
ROGER DEAN
ILLUSTRATION
ROGER DEAN

NEVERMIND

NIRVANA

LABEL
GEFFEN
ART DIRECTION
ROBERT FISHER
DESIGN
ROBERT FISHER
COVER
PHOTOGRAPHY
KIRK WEDDLE
OTHER
PHOTOGRAPHY
MICHAEL LAVINE

TECHNIQUE
NEW ORDER

LABEL
QWEST
COVER DESIGN
**PETER SAVILLE
ASSOCIATES
TREVOR KEY**

DREAM
TUCK & PATTI

LABEL
WINDHAM HILL
ART DIRECTION
JENNIFER MORLA
DESIGN
JENNIFER MORLA
JEANETTE
ARAMBURU
PHOTOGRAPHER
GERALD BYBEE/
BYBEE STUDIOS
COPYWRITER
WINDHAM HILL

OUT OF TIME

R.E.M.

LABEL

WARNER BROTHERS

ART DIRECTION

TOM RECCHION

MICHAEL STIPE

DESIGN

TOM RECCHION

MICHAEL STIPE

BAND PHOTOGRAPHY

FRANK OCKENFELS

OTHER
PHOTOGRAPHY

PLANT DETAILS #3:
YELLOW SEASCAPE
WITH FILM AND
WOOD BLOCK

**DOUG & MIKE
STARN**

ED ROGERS

**DAVID
GREENBERGER/
DUPLEX PLANET**

ILLUSTRATION

BEN KATCHOR

HAND LETTERING

ED ROGERS

COMPUTER
GRAPHICS

TOM RECCHION

COLLAGE

TOM RECCHION

MICHAEL STIPE

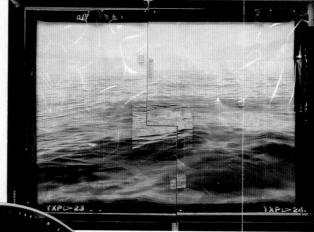

RADIO SONG
LOSING MY RELIGION
LOW
NEAR WILD HEAVEN
DG
SHINY HAPPY PEOPLE
R G
HALF A WORLD AWAY
XARKAN
COUNT   FDBACK
ME IN HONEY

R.E.M. OUT OF TIME

R.E.M. OUT OF TIME

9 26496-2

, MICHAEL STIPE [AND] BERTIS E. DOWNS, IV. W. PETER HOLSAPPLE, KIDD JORDAN, KRS-1, KATE NT. MARK BINGHAM. **ORCHESTRAL LIAISON**: MPERS–VIOLIN, DAVID BRAITBERG–VIOLIN, DAVID HARRIS–VIOLA, PAUL MURPHY–VIOLA & LEADER, , RALPH JONES–DOUBLE BASS. **HORN PLAYERS**: ONES, BASS CLARINET; CECIL WELCH–FLUGELHORN. **M ASSISTANCE**: BILL THOMSON. **OFFICE** CK, E.M. CARTER. **PRODUCED** BY SCOTT LITT & **TRACKS RECORDED** AT BEARSVILLE STUDIOS, IKE REITER. **COORDINATION** IAN KIMMET. STUDIOS, GEORGIA; **ENGINEER** JOHN KEANE. DIOS, GEORGIA; **ASSISTANT ENGINEER** TED MINNESOTA **ASSISTANT ENGINEERS** DAVE ON: DEBORAH WANG. **MASTERED** BY STEPHEN IA. **PACKAGING & ARTWORK DIRECTION** Y: **SINGLE PANELS** BEN KATCHOR; PICTURE– W NO. 2: PASSERSBY FRANK OCKENFELS; BAND SONG TITLES; R.E.M. LOGO; KARINA SANTOS: PHOTOGRAPH: PLANT DETAILS #3, PHOTOGRAPH: CKS: **INTERAGENT TO ED ROGERS** DAVID NT TO BEN KATCHOR JEM COHEN. **RADIO** TAR; MIKE–ORGAN, BASS; MICHAEL–VOCALS; KRS– ARK BINGHAM–STRING ARRANGEMENT; KIDD ES; SCOTT LITT–ECHO-LOOP FEED. **LOSING MY**

RELIGION: BILL–DRUMS, PERCUSSION; PETER–MANDOLIN, ELECTRIC OCTAVE GUITAR; MIKE–BASS, VOCALS, KEYBOARD STRINGS & ARRANGEMENT; MICHAEL–VOCALS; PETER HOLSAPPLE–ACOUSTIC GUITAR. **LOW**: BILL–CONGAS, PERCUSSION; PETER–GUITAR; MIKE–ORGAN; MICHAEL–VOCALS; PETER HOLSAPPLE–BASS; MARK BINGHAM–STRING ARRANGEMENT; KIDD JORDAN–BASS CLARINET. **NEAR WILD HEAVEN**: BILL–DRUMS, PERCUSSION, VOCALS, PIANO; PETER–GUITARS; MIKE–BASS, VOCALS; MICHAEL–VOCALS, MARK BINGHAM–STRING ARRANGEMENT; KIDD JORDAN–BARITONE SAXOPHONE. **ENDGAME**: BILL–PERCUSSION; PETER–ACOUSTIC & ELECTRIC GUITAR; MIKE–BASS, ORGAN; MICHAEL–VOCALS, BASS MELODICA, STRING & HORN ARRANGEMENT, MARK BINGHAM–STRING ARRANGEMENT; KIDD JORDAN–BASS CLARINET; TENOR SAXOPHONE; CECIL WELCH–FLUGELHORN. **SHINY HAPPY PEOPLE**: BILL–DRUMS, PERCUSSION; PETER–ELECTRIC GUITAR; MIKE–ORGAN, BASS, VOCALS; MICHAEL–VOCALS; KATE PIERSON–VOCALS; PETER HOLSAPPLE–ACOUSTIC GUITAR; MARK BINGHAM–STRING ARRANGEMENT. **BELONG**: BILL–DRUMS, VOCALS, PERCUSSION; PETER–ELECTRIC GUITAR; MIKE–BASS, VOCALS, PIANO; MICHAEL–VOCALS; PETER HOLSAPPLE–ELECTRIC GUITAR. **HALF A WORLD AWAY**: BILL–BASS, PERCUSSION; PETER–MANDOLIN, ACOUSTIC GUITAR; MIKE–ORGAN, HARPSICHORD, VOCALS, PERCUSSION; MICHAEL–VOCALS; MARK BINGHAM–STRING ARRANGEMENT. **TEXARKANA**: BILL–DRUMS, PERCUSSION; PETER–ELECTRIC GUITAR; MIKE–BASS, VOCALS; KEYBOARD STRINGS & ARRANGEMENT; MICHAEL–VOCALS; PETER HOLSAPPLE–ACOUSTIC GUITAR; JOHN KEANE–PEDAL STEEL GUITAR; MARK BINGHAM–STRING ARRANGEMENT. **COUNTRY FEEDBACK**: BILL–DRUMS, PERCUSSION, VOCALS; PETER–ACOUSTIC GUITAR, LOUD GUITAR; MIKE–ORGAN; MICHAEL–VOCALS; KATE PIERSON–VOCALS; JOHN KEANE–PEDAL STEEL GUITAR. **ME IN HONEY**: BILL–DRUMS, PERCUSSION; PETER–GUITAR; MIKE–BASS; MICHAEL–VOCALS; KATE PIERSON–VOCALS. **ALL SONGS** BERRY, BUCK, MILLS, STIPE. **PUBLISHED** BY NIGHT GARDEN MUSIC, ADMINISTERED EVERYWHERE BY UNICHAPPELL MUSIC, INC. BMI. KATE PIERSON APPEARS COURTESY OF REPRISE RECORDS. KRS-1 APPEARS COURTESY OF JIVE RECORDS. ©1991 R.E.M./ATHENS, LTD. MADE IN U.S.A.

DEADICATED

DEADICATED
VARIOUS ARTISTS

LABEL
ARISTA
BOOKLET DESIGN
ANN PETTER
ILLUSTRATION
MIKIO/WILLIAM GIESE
TREE BARK PHOTO
W. CODY/ WESTLIGHT

LILY ON THE BEACH

TANGERINE DREAM

LABEL

PRIVATE MUSIC

COVER ART

NORMAN MOORE

DESIGN

NORMAN MOORE

PHOTOGRAPHY

IAN LOGAN

PHOTO CONCEPT

MONICA FROESE

PHOTO ART

DIRECTION

**HEIDI
BAUMGARTEN**

OPTICAL RACE

TANGERINE DREAM

LABEL

PRIVATE MUSIC

ART DIRECTION

NORMAN MOORE

DESIGN

NORMAN MOORE

COVER CONCEPT

MONICA FROESE

ABSOLUT(E)

CLAUDIA BRUCKEN

LABEL

ISLAND

PHOTOGRAPHY

**DOUGLAS
BROTHERS**

RED HOT & BLUE
VARIOUS ARTISTS

LABEL
CHRYSALIS
ART DIRECTION
HELENE SILVERMAN
DESIGN
FRANK GARGIULO

FRANCESCA BEGHÈ

FRANCESCA BEGHÈ

LABEL

SBK

ART DIRECTION

**MANHATTAN
DESIGN**

PHOTOGRAPHY

**MANHATTAN
DESIGN**

FRANCESCA BEGHÈ

FRANCESCA BEGHÈ

LABEL

SBK

ART DIRECTION

**MANHATTAN
DESIGN**

PHOTOGRAPHY

**MANHATTAN
DESIGN**

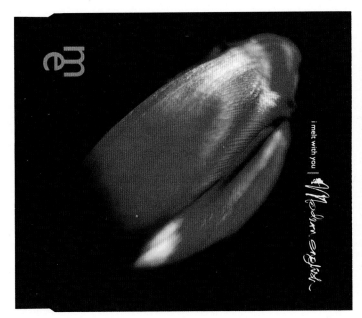

I MELT WITH YOU

MODERN ENGLISH

LABEL

TVT

ART DIRECTION

VAUGHAN OLIVER/v23

DESIGN

VAUGHAN OLIVER/v23

PHOTOGRAPHY

DOMINIC DAVIES

CALLIGRAPHY

CHRIS BIGG

PILLOW LIPS

MODERN ENGLISH

LABEL

TVT

ART DIRECTION

VAUGHAN OLIVER/v23

DESIGN

VAUGHAN OLIVER/v23

PHOTOGRAPHY

DOMINIC DAVIES

MARCUS GRAHAM

CALLIGRAPHY

CHRIS BIGG

TROMPE LE MONDE

PIXIES

LABEL

ELECTRA

ART DIRECTION & DESIGN

VAUGHAN OLIVIER/ v23

PHOTOGRAPHY

SIMON LARBALESTIER

ROCKETS

STEVEN APPLEBY

BOSSONOVA

PIXIES

LABEL

ELECTRA

ART DIRECTION & DESIGN

VAUGHAN OLIVIER/ v23

PHOTOGRAPHY

SIMON LARBALESTIER

PORTRAIT

KEVIN WESTENBERG

DESIGN ASSISTANCE

CHRIS BIGG

GLOBE

PIRATE DESIGN

VELOURIA'S OUTFIT

ANNE GARRIGUES

BELLYBUTTON
JELLYFISH

LABEL
CHARISMA
ART DIRECTION
STEVE SAMIOF
DESIGN
MICK HAGGERTY
PHOTOGRAPHY
**PETER DARLEY
MILLER**

BABY'S COMING BACK
JELLYFISH

LABEL
CHARISMA
ART DIRECTION
STEVE SAMIOF
DESIGN
RON MECKLER
PHOTOGRAPHY
**PETER DARLEY
MILLER**

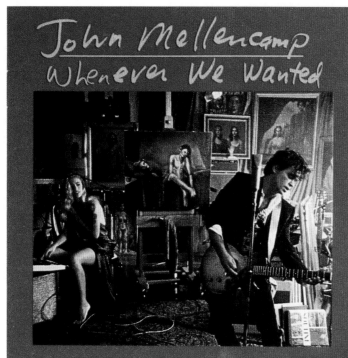

WHENEVER WE
WANTED

JOHN MELLENCAMP

LABEL
POLYGRAM
ART DIRECTION
**CORSILLO/
MANZONE**
PHOTOGRAPHY
WAYNE MASER
PAINTINGS
JOHN MELLENCAMP

FAMILY STYLE
**VAUGHAN
BROTHERS**

LABEL
EPIC
ART DIRECTION
TONY SELLARI
PHOTOGRAPHY
LEE CRUM

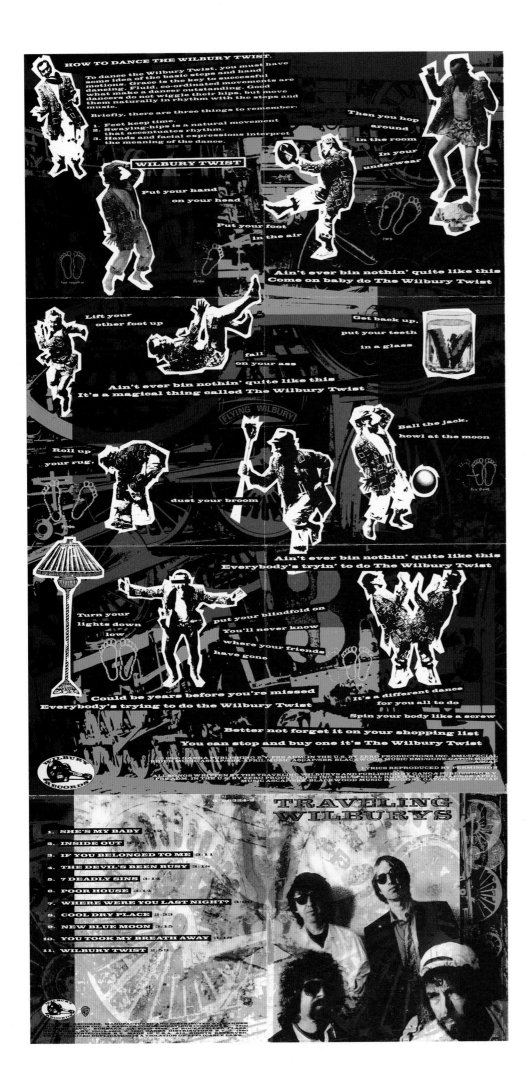

VOL. 3

TRAVELING WILBURYS

LABEL

WARNER BROTHERS

ART DIRECTION

DAVID COSTA & NICKY HAMES FOR WHEREFORE ART

DESIGN

DAVID COSTA & NICKY HAMES FOR WHEREFORE ART

PHOTOGRAPHY

CAROLINE GREYSHOCK

JULIAN HAKINS

The insert for this CD includes a fold-out illustrating the dance steps described in the song "Wilbury Twist."

PUMP UP THE JAM
TECHOTRONIC

LABEL
SBK
DESIGN
JANET PERR

TRIP ON THIS
TECHNOTRONIC

LABEL
TECHNOTRONIC
ART DIRECTION
**MANHATTAN
DESIGN**
PHOTOGRAPHY
ELLEN CAREY

Digital and Analog Multi-Track Recording:
GRAMAVISION STUDIO, NYC (ERIC LILJESTRAND—engineer)
AXIS PRODUCTIONS, NYC (FRANCOIS KEVORKIAN—engineer)
THE LIVING ROOM, NYC (BLAISE DUPUY—engineer)
ACTIVE RECORDING, NYC (STEVE TJADEN—engineer)
CEDAR SOUND, NYC (ERIC LILJESTRAND—engineer)
CIANI/MUSICA, NYC (ERIC LILJESTRAND—engineer)

Pre-Production & MIDI Recording:
STUDIO PASS, NYC (CAROL PARKINSON, CONNIE KIELTYKA and
ALEX GARDNER—engineers)
GRACIE'S, BALDWIN, NY (DAVID LEBOLT—engineer)
EFFANEL MUSIC, NYC (JOHN HARRIS—engineer)
ROSEWOOD SOUND, BROOKLYN, NY (DAVID VAN TIEGHEM)

Mixed by DAVID VAN TIEGHEM, BLAISE DUPUY and PAUL RICE at
The Living Room, NYC, except "Strange Cargo," mixed at Axis Productions, NYC by
FRANCOIS KEVORKIAN and DAVID VAN TIEGHEM

Assistant Engineers—TIM CASEY (Gramavision), MICHAEL McGRATH (Living Room)
ALAN FRIEDMAN, RODNEY ASCUE, BILL ESSES (Axis); JAMES
LA CROIX, JEFFREY SHORE (Ciani/Musica); ED McKINLEY (Active)

Recorded using Macintosh SE and Macintosh II computers, running Mark of the Unicorn's Performer,
Opcode Systems' Vision and Sequencer, and Digidesign's Sound Tools software.

Pre-production and arranging assistance—ROMA BARAN and DAVID LEBOLT
Additional arranging assistance—PAUL RICE

Mastered by PHIL AUSTIN at TRUTONE RECORDS, Haworth, NJ

All selections written by DAVID VAN TIEGHEM (published by BOOMER MUSIC/ASCAP)
except "Hell or High Water" and "Volcano Diving," music by DAVID VAN TIEGHEM and
DAVID LEBOLT, lyrics by DAVID VAN TIEGHEM
ASCAP and LONG MARCH MUSIC/BMI)   (published by BOOMER MUSIC

Mark Egan appears courtesy of GRP Records.

THE CREATIVE INPUT OF ALL THE PARTICIPANTS ON THIS
RECORDING IS GRATEFULLY ACKNOWLEDGED.

Art Director MARK LARSON
Art Coordinator TISH FRIED
Photography by PENNY GENTIEU

For TINA…

MANY THANKS TO THE FOLLOWING INDIVIDUALS AND ORGANIZATIONS WITHOUT WHOSE
SUPPORT AND ASSISTANCE THIS PROJECT WOULD NOT HAVE BEEN POSSIBLE

STRANGE CARGO
DAVID VAN TIEGHEM

LABEL
PRIVATE MUSIC
ART DIRECTION
MARK LARSON
ART COORDINATOR
TISH FRIED
PHOTOGRAPHY
PENNY GENTIEU

THE ULTIMATE CREATION
RAPPINSTINE

LABEL
WARNER BROS./ QWEST
ART DIRECTION
TOM RECCHION
DESIGN
KEVIN DESIGN HOSMANN
PHOTOGRAPHY
ROCKY SCHENCK
SET DESIGN
KELLY REY

FOLLOW FOR NOW
FOLLOW FOR NOW

LABEL
CHRYSALIS
ART DIRECTION
MANHATTAN DESIGN
DESIGN
MANHATTAN DESIGN
ILLUSTRATION
MATT MAHURIN
PHOTOGRAPHY
RUTH LEITMAN JANETTE BECKMAN

I FOUND OUT

THE CHRISTIANS

LABEL
ISLAND
ART DIRECTION
MAINLINE ART
ISLAND ART
DESIGN
MAINLINE ART
ISLAND ART
PHOTOGRAPHY
ALISTAIR THAIN

THE ODD GET EVEN

SHADOWFAX

LABEL
PRIVATE MUSIC
ART DIRECTION
NORMAN MOORE
DESIGN
NORMAN MOORE
PHOTOGRAPHY
MERLYN ROSENBERG

THE RED HOUSE

THE RED HOUSE

LABEL
SBK
ART DIRECTION
MARK LARSON
PHOTOGRAPHY
CAROLINE GREYSHOCK

The Acoustic Music Project is a collective of San Francisco musicians and individuals working together to document and promote the local new acoustic music scene, while at the same time generating funds for the AIDS "meals on wheels" organization, Project Open Hand. The album was recorded live at the historic Great American Music Hall, and at various recording studios throughout the Bay Area. Each of the artists included on the record have generously donated their time, talent and royalties to this project. The committee warmly thanks each and every artist for their contribution.

For more information on A.M.P. or to make a donation to Project Open Hand, please write: Acoustic Music Project, c/o Project Open Hand, 2727 - 17th Street, San Francisco, CA., 94110

A.M.P. Committee / Executive Producers
Ron Gompertz, Founder
Barry Simons, Esq.
Nadine Condon
Lorry Fleming
Chris L. Mitchell
Pat Thomas
Jim English
Oliver DiCicco

*ACOUSTIC MUSIC
PROJECT*

LABEL
ALIAS RECORDS
ART DIRECTION
**FRANK
WIEDERMANN**
DESIGN
**FRANK
WIEDERMANN**
PHOTOGRAPHY
**FRANK
WIEDERMANN**
LOGO
SUE HUTNER

ACOUSTIC MUSIC PROJECT

• AMERICAN MUSIC CLUB • BARTON, DARLINGTON, & DEKKER • CONNIE CHAMPAGNE • ALEX CHILTON •
• NANCIE DE ROSS • ED HAYNES • J. C. HOPKINS • PENELOPE HOUSTON • SONYA HUNTER •
• BARBARA MANNING • THE MOVIE STARS • THE MUSKRATS • EDDIE RAY PORTER •
• CHUCK PROPHET & STEPHANIE FINCH • JONATHAN SEGEL • JERRY SHELFER • THE SNEETCHES •
• DANNY SORENTINO • PATRICK WINNINGHAM • STEPHEN YERKEY •

ON COMPACT DISC AND CASSETTE

Sales benefit Project Open Hand,
"Meals With Love for People With AIDS"

374 Branman St., San Francisco CA 94107   •   10153 1/2 Riverside Dr., #115 Toluca Lake CA 91602

COLOR HARMONY

A step-by-step guide to choosing and combining colors, **Color Harmony** includes 1,662 individual color combinations; dozens of full-color photos to show you how your color schemes will look; a four-color conversion chart; 61 full-size charts and much more.

158 pages   *Softcover*
$15.95   *ISBN 0-935603-06-9*

MIX & MATCH DESIGNER'S COLORS

Produced by a designer for designers, this book incorporates several features aimed at minimizing guesswork and eliminating errors that are often experienced when using traditional methods of choosing tints for us in four-color process. Extra large swatches show the color extremely clearly, and the ability to turn them over individually allows colors to be compared. From each swatch, the designer can see a variety of color percentages, how both knock out and overprint type will appear on that tint, and also how a halftone image appears printed in that color.

300 swatches   *Hardcover*
$34.95   *ISBN 1-56496-009-9*

GRAPHIC IDEA NOTEBOOK

The new revised softcover edition of this workhorse book contains 24 all-new pages. This book is a study in graphic design, covering innovative problem-solving, demonstrating techniques to turn routine material into provocative editorial presentation.

216 pages   *Softcover*
$18.95   *ISBN 0-935603-64-6*

THE BEST OF NEON

THE BEST OF NEON is an exciting, encompassing survey of the top current designs in neon Featured are more than 400 full-color designs and 256 pages of innovative applications. Major sections are devoted to Architecture, Interiors, and Signs. Included are examples of neon creativity... sophisticated, dramatic, subdued, humorous, snappy or bold

256 pages   *Hardcover*
$59.95   *ISBN 0-935603-60-3*

NEW & NOTABLE PRODUCT DESIGN

In recent years there have been tremendous advances in American and international contemporary design. New materials and more compact technology have yielded many new designs, and NEW & NOTABLE PRODUCT DESIGN is a showcase for these innovative products. Many of the products in this book have been recognized by awards for their designs. A valuable sourcebook for home or office.

256 pages   *Hardcover*
$49.95   *ISBN 0-935603-62-X*

DESKTOP PUBLISHER'S EASY TYPE GUIDE
The 150 Most Important Typefaces

There are thousands of different type styles available to the owners of desktop publishing systems, and more being created daily. How does one choose which to purchase? This book will not only help you make those decisions, but will show you how to get the most benefit from the type styles you choose. From the neophyte designer, to the desktop newcomer this guide will prove a valuable resource.

176 pages   *Softcover*
$19.95   *ISBN 1-56496-007-2*

GRAPHIC DESIGN NEW YORK

This book celebrates the wealth of design talent in New York by featuring the work of the top 40 New York City design firms and individual designers. Also included are essays by Steven Heller, creative director of the New York Times; Milton Glaser; designer Paula Scher; Tibor Kalman of Interview magazine; and Colin Forbes of Pentagram. The work, featured in magnificent full color, represents the best in corporate, information, and consumer design.

336 pages   *Hardcover*
$49.95   *ISBN 0-935603-62-X*

TYPE & COLOR:
A Handbook of Creative Combinations

Graphic artists must perform quickly, creatively and accurately. **Type & Color** enables graphic artists to spec type in color quickly and efficiently. Ten sheets of color type styles printed on acetate overlays can be combined with hundreds of color bars, making it possible to experiment with thousands of color/type combinations right at the drawing board. In minutes, your eye will rapidly judge what the mind had conceived. 160 pages plus 10 pages of acetate overlays.

160 pages   *Hardcover*
$34.95   *ISBN 0-935603-19-0*

TYPE IN PLACE
A Thumbnail Approach to Creative Type Placement

This companion guide to **Type & Color** includes 11 acetates with printed type for use with thumbnail images in the book. With this tool, designers can easily envision in thumbnail, ideas for type placement with sample layouts included in the text. This new system allows designers to start from scratch in designing type placements rather than to start from the point of imitation. 60 pages of examples of great type placements are also included.

160 pages   *Hardcover*
$39.95   *ISBN 0-935603-87-5*

Volume One:
TRADEMARKS & SYMBOLS OF THE WORLD: THE ALPHABET IN DESIGN

This wonderful idea book presents more than 1,700 contemporary designs for every letter of the alphabet. An essential resource for anyone who designs logos and corporate identities.

192 pages   *Softcover*
$24.95   *ISBN 4-7601-0451-8*

Volume Two:
TRADEMARKS & SYMBOLS OF THE WORLD: DESIGN ELEMENTS

If you design packages, ads, corporate logos or signage, you must have this resource guide in your design library. It features more than 1,700 design elements that can add pizzazz to any printed piece.

192 pages   *Softcover*
$24.95   *ISBN 4-7601-0450-X*

Volume Three:
TRADEMARKS & SYMBOLS OF THE WORLD: PICTOGRAM & SIGN DESIGN

This book is packed with 1,800 pictogram and sign designs from all over the world. They were selected for their unique ability to nonverbally convey a message: no left turn, clothes must be worn here, flammable, camel crossing, beware, volcanic activity, eclairs available, I Love You - and 1793 more.

232 pages   *Softcover*
$24.95   *ISBN 0-935603-30-1*

Volume Four:
TRADEMARKS & SYMBOLS OF THE WORLD: EUROPEAN TRADEMARKS COLLECTION

Volume 4 presents over 2000 logos and symbols from all over Europe. A wide variety of industries are represented, and there's a handy glossary in the back. An essential idea book for any graphic artist involved in developing logos and corporate identities.

216 pages   *Softcover*
$24.95   *ISBN 1-56496-019-6*

3- DIMENSIONAL ILLUSTRATORS AWARDS ANNUAL II
The Best in 3-D Advertising and Publishing Worldwide

This state-of-the-art sourcebook is dedicated exclusively to the use of 3-dimensional illustration. It includes the latest series of full-color 3-dimensional illustrations from the Second Annual Dimensional Awards show. The 3-D effect is achieved through paper sculpture, clay sculpture, fabric collage, wood sculpture, plastic sculpture, mixed media, and singular mediums.

256 pages   *Hardcover*
$59.95   *ISBN 0-935603-89-1*